· Bartholomew ·

EDINBURGH
ILLUSTRATED ATLAS

Designed and
researched by
Dominic Beddow

Illustrated by
Joanna Canessa

DATES IN EDINBURGH'S HISTORY

	The earliest signs of permanent settlement in the area are burial remains found along the Water of Leith. They date back to around 2000 B.C. There are the sites of several Iron Age forts around the city.
c.142	Fort built by Romans at Cramond
626	Edinburgh founded by Edwin of Northumbria. 'Dun Eideann' is Gaelic for 'fortress of the hill slope'
638	Edinburgh fell to the Bernicians (northern English) under Oswald
1018	Malcolm II's victory over the Northumbrians at Carham confirmed Edinburgh as a Scottish town
1128	Abbey at Holyrood founded by David I (1124-53)
1295	Treaty signed with France - beginning of 'Auld Alliance'
1296	Castle sacked in punishment by Edward I's English army
1322	Holyrood Abbey sacked by English
1368	Rebuilding of Castle started - it begins to take on its modern form
1376	Population of the city was about 2000
1498	Palace of Holyroodhouse founded
1482	Edinburgh occupied by Richard of Gloucester
1544	Leith and city burned by invading English under Edward Seymour on the orders of Henry VIII. Leith razed a second time in 1547
1560	Treaty of Edinburgh: ousted French abandoned any claim to Scotland
1582	Edinburgh University founded
1645	Great Plague kills two-thirds of Leith
1603	Royal court moves to London
1658	First stage-coach to London
1681	Royal College of Physicians founded
1693	Law restricted throwing of slops and rubbish to between 10 p.m. and 6 a.m.
1695	Bank of Scotland founded by Act of Parliament. Also the time of the first public concert in the city
1707	Act of Union moves power to Westminster
1726	Allan Ramsay founded first lending library
1727	Royal Bank of Scotland founded
1737	Edinburgh was fined for allowing a mob to lynch Captain Porteus during riots in the previous year
1745	The Fortyfive: Bonnie Prince Charlie took Edinburgh and defeated the British army at Preston Pans, before being beaten at Culloden in 1746
1750-1800	The Scottish Enlightenment: the economist Adam Smith, the philosopher David Hume and others active in Edinburgh
1752	Proposal to build New Town
1760s	Nor' Loch drained (now Princes Street Gardens)
1767-1810	Building of First New Town
1782	Act of Proscription repealed. End of restrictions on kilt wearing imposed after the Fortyfive
1801-30	Planning and building of Northern New Town
1820s	Moray estate (around Moray Place) developed. Façades designed by Gillespie Graham
1831	Thomas Telford's Dean Bridge opened - allowed development of Dean estate and other westward expansion
1833	John Menzies opened his first book shop. James Thin opened in 1848
1838	City Agreement Act made Leith a separate municipality
1846	Railway route to London opened through Princes Street Gardens
1856	Canongate becomes a part of Edinburgh rather than a separate burgh
1920	Similarly, Leith becomes a part of Edinburgh
1928	Establishment of Scottish Office as the Government administrative department for Scotland
1947	First Edinburgh Festival
1966	Heriot-Watt University founded

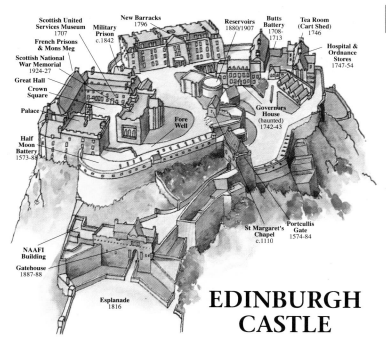

Scottish United Services Museum 1707
French Prisons & Mons Meg
Scottish National War Memorial 1924-27
Great Hall
Crown Square
Palace
Half Moon Battery 1573-88
New Barracks 1796
Military Prison c.1842
Fore Well
Reservoirs 1880/1907
Butts Battery 1708-1713
Tea Room (Cart Shed) 1746
Hospital & Ordnance Stores 1747-54
Governors House (haunted) 1742-43
St Margaret's Chapel c.1110
Portcullis Gate 1574-84
NAAFI Building
Gatehouse 1887-88
Esplanade 1816

EDINBURGH CASTLE

There has been a fort of some kind on this massive rock since around the year 600. The earliest surviving part of the Castle is St Margaret's Chapel, dating from around 1110. The Castle in its present form is therefore the result of nearly 900 years of demolition, destruction, rebuilding and expansion. In that time the Castle has served all purposes. It is most obviously a fortress, being almost unassailable from three sides - when the Castle has fallen, it has done so through lack of food or water, not because of a direct assault. It has also been an ordnance factory, a place of worship, barracks, record office, treasury, prison and royal residence. Pictish Kings used the site to store their women. It was known, perhaps inappropriately, as 'The Castle of the Virgins'.

In the sixteenth century a foundry was built and the Castle developed as an arsenal and munitions factory. This made it less suitable as a royal home and in 1542 the newly crowned Mary Queen of Scots moved to Holyrood.

In medieval times an army would only be raised if needed. The seventeenth century saw the growth in Scotland of a standing, professional army to protect the interests of British monarchs who were seldom there. The Castle became predominantly a military base and is still the headquarters of the Scottish Division.

Particular things to see:

The Palace: a much modified 15/16th century building. The north half was re-designed for James VI (I of England) in 1615-17. Contains **Mary's Bedroom**, where the same James VI was born in 1566, the **Great Hall** (built in 1433, restored in 1887-91) and the **Crown Room,** in which are stored the Scottish Honours: crown, sceptre and sword of state. You can also see the oak chest they were in when they were lost for over 100 years.

French Prisons: up to 1000 'P.O.W.s' were kept here during the Napoleonic Wars. Now houses Mons Meg, a five ton siege gun forged in 1449.

Scottish United Services Museum: good collection of highland weaponry.

Scottish National War Memorial: fine stained glass, flags and a memorial shrine commemorate those Scots who died in the First World War.

One O'Clock Gun: fired as a time signal for ships each weekday since 1851.

CAMERA
OBSCURA
Outlook
Tower

Ramsay Lane

Boswell's
Court

Tolbooth Kirk (St Johns) Octagonal spire is the highest in the city. Rich in Gothic detail. Finished in 1844

Site of Edinburgh's earliest municipal reservoir, creating water pressure for buildings on the hill. This one, built in 1849, can hold two million gallons.

Reservoir

Cannonball House

Castle Wynd West

A ball is stuck in the west gable. One story is that it was fired from the Castle but apparently this defies ballistics. Alternatively, it marked the highest point to which water could be provided.

A tunnel was found which was thought to run from the Castle to Holyrood. A bagpiper went down to explore, piping away so that people could follow his progress. Half way down the tune stopped, he was never see again, though it is said you can sometimes hear him faintly

Good view of Nor' Loch and Princes Street

View to Grassmarket and Heriot's School

H6   H7
H7   G7

Scene of the annual Military Tattoo. The steep slope to the castle was flattened in the 1850 using rubble from the City Chambers foundations. This parade ground was completed in 1816

Esplanade

Dry

Ditch

Half
Moon
Battery

Portcullis
Gate

Crown
Room

Palace

Argyle Battery

St Margaret's
Chapel

Scottish National
War Memorial

Crown
Square

Great Hall

Scottish United
Services Museum

Old Governor's
House

New Barracks

ROYAL MILE

0   50   100
        Yards

Pages 8 to 11 follow the Royal Mile from west to east.
Shops and further notes on the route are shown on the main map (pages 42, 43, 44 and 37).

A walk down this historic route between the Castle and Holyroodhouse takes you through the heart of the the old burghs of Edinburgh and Canongate. Until the eighteenth century the city extended, at most, half a mile either side of the Royal Mile, and the inhabitants sought the protection of the Castle in buildings jumbled up on top of one another, interweaved with narrow 'wynds' or alleyways.
As the city expanded down the hill the buildings became less congested, and the Mile ends near the open spaces of Holyrood Park. A comparison of the Castle at one end and Holyroodhouse at the other, shows how Renaissance thinking throughout Europe changed royal palaces from being sources of power to symbols of prestige.
The Royal Mile traces a path through history from the time when Scotland was a harsh, medieval, subsistence economy, to the beginning of the enlightened era which produced the elegant terraces of Southside and the New Town.

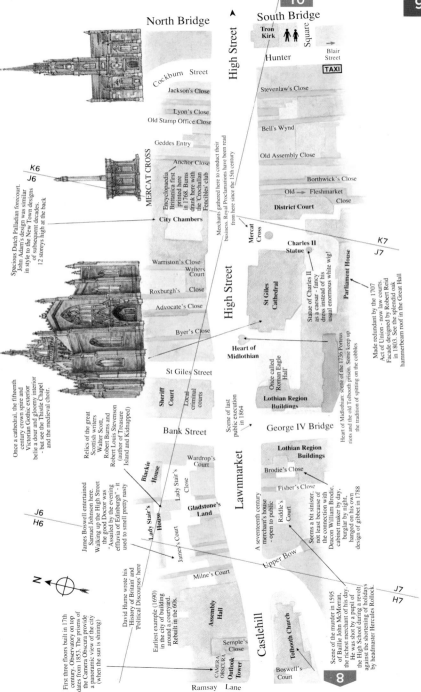

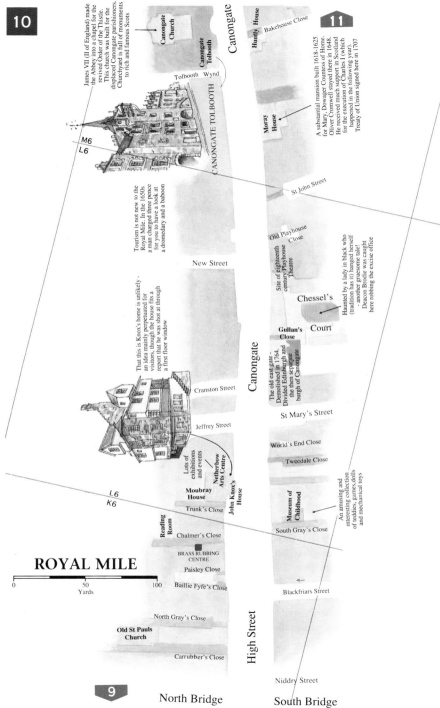

Canongate

James VII (II of England) made the Abbey into a chapel for the revived Order of the Thistle. This church was built for the displaced Canongate parishioners. Churchyard is full of monuments to rich and famous Scots

Canongate Church

Canongate Tolbooth

Tolbooth Wynd

Huntly House

Bakehouse Close

A substantial mansion built 1618-1625 for Mary, Dowager Countess of Home. Oliver Cromwell stayed there in 1648. He received much support in Scotland for the execution of Charles I (which happened in the following year). Treaty of Union signed here in 1707

Moray House

CANONGATE TOLBOOTH

M6
L6

St John Street

Tourism is not new to the Royal Mile. In the 1650s a man charged three pence for you to have a look at a dromedary and a baboon

New Street

Old Playhouse Close

Site of eighteenth century Playhouse Theatre

Chessel's Court

Haunted by a lady in black who (tradition has it) hanged herself - another gruesome tale! Deacon Brodie was caught here robbing the excise office

That this is Knox's home is unlikely - an idea mainly perpetuated for visitors, although the house fits a report that he was shot at through a first floor window

Gullan's Close

The old east gate - Demolished in 1764. Divided Edinburgh and the then separate burgh of Canongate

Cranston Street

Canongate

St Mary's Street

Jeffrey Street

World's End Close

Tweedale Close

Lots of exhibitions and events

Netherbow Arts Centre

Moubray House

John Knox's House

Museum of Childhood

An amusing and interesting collection of teddies, games, dolls and mechanical toys

L6
K6

Trunk's Close

South Gray's Close

Reading Room

Chalmer's Close

ROYAL MILE

BRASS RUBBING CENTRE

Paisley Close

Blackfriars Street

0   50   100
         Yards

Baillie Fyfe's Close

North Gray's Close

High Street

Old St Pauls Church

Carrubber's Close

Niddry Street

North Bridge

South Bridge

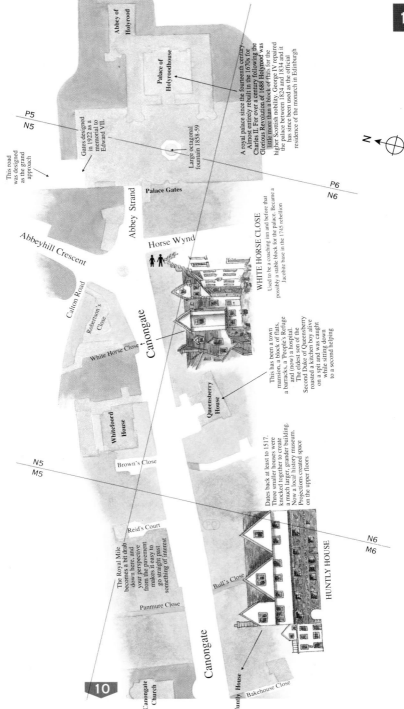

Abbey of Holyrood

Palace of Holyroodhouse

A royal palace since the fourteenth century. Almost entirely rebuilt in the 1670s for Charles II. For over a century following the Glorious Revolution of 1688 Holyrood was little more than a block of flats for the higher Scottish nobility. George IV repaired the palace between 1824 and 1834 and it has since been used as the official residence of the monarch in Edinburgh

P5
N5

Gates designed in 1922 as a memorial to Edward VII.

This road was designed as the grand approach

Large octagonal fountain 1858-59

P6
N6

N

Abbey Strand

Palace Gates

Abbeyhill Crescent

Horse Wynd

WHITE HORSE CLOSE
Used to be a coaching inn and before that the stables for the palace. Became a possibly a stable block for the palace. Became a Jacobite base in the 1745 rebellion

Calton Road

Canongate

Robertson's Close

White Horse Close

This has been a town mansion, a block of flats, a barracks, a 'People's Refuge' and (now) a hospital. The eldest son of the Second Duke of Queensberry roasted a kitchen boy alive on a spit and was caught while sitting down to a second helping

Whiteford House

Queensberry House

Brown's Close

N5
M5

Reid's Court

Dates back at least to 1517. Three smaller houses were knocked together to create a much larger, grander building. Now a local history museum. Projections created space on the upper floors

The Royal Mile becomes a bit drab down here, and your perspective from the pavement makes it easy to go straight past something of interest

N6
M6

HUNTLY HOUSE

Panmure Close

Bull's Close

Canongate

Huntly House

Bakehouse Close

Canongate Church

KEY:

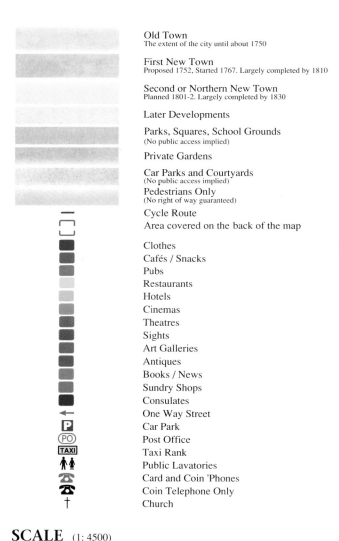

Old Town
The extent of the city until about 1750

First New Town
Proposed 1752, Started 1767. Largely completed by 1810

Second or Northern New Town
Planned 1801-2. Largely completed by 1830

Later Developments

Parks, Squares, School Grounds
(No public access implied)

Private Gardens

Car Parks and Courtyards
(No public access implied)

Pedestrians Only
(No right of way guaranteed)

Cycle Route

Area covered on the back of the map

Clothes
Cafés / Snacks
Pubs
Restaurants
Hotels
Cinemas
Theatres
Sights
Art Galleries
Antiques
Books / News
Sundry Shops
Consulates
One Way Street
Car Park
Post Office
Taxi Rank
Public Lavatories
Card and Coin 'Phones
Coin Telephone Only
Church

SCALE (1: 4500)
1 Kilometre = approx. 20cm
1 Mile = approx. 14 inches

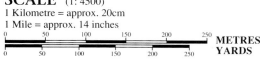

METRES
YARDS

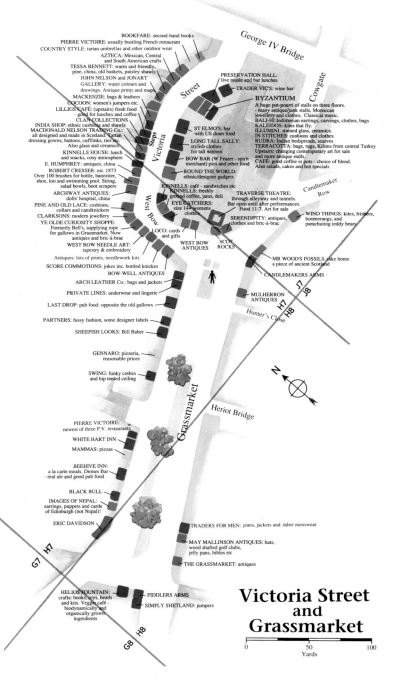

BOOKFARE: second-hand books
PIERRE VICTOIRE: usually bustling French restaurant
COUNTRY STYLE: tartan umbrellas and other outdoor wear
AZTECA: Mexican, Central and South American crafts
TESSA BENNETT: warm and friendly, pine, china, old baskets, paisley shawls
JOHN NELSON and JONART GALLERY: water colours and drawings. Antique prints and map
MACKENZIE: bags & leathers
COCOON: women's jumpers etc.
LILLIGS CAFÉ: (upstairs) fresh food - good for lunches and coffee
CLAN COLLECTIONS
INDIA SHOP: ethnic cushions and shawls
MACDONALD NELSON TRADING Co.: all designed and made in Scotland. Tartan dressing gowns, buttons, cufflinks, ties etc. Also glass and ceramics.
KINNELLS HOUSE: lunch and snacks, cosy atmosphere
E. HUMPHREY: antiques, china
ROBERT CRESSER: est. 1873 Over 100 brushes for bottle, bannister, shoe, loo and swimming pool. String, salad bowls, boot scrapers
ARCHWAY ANTIQUES: dolls' hospital, china
PINE AND OLD LACE: cushions, collars and camiknickers
CLARKSONS: modern jewellery
YE OLDE CURIOSITY SHOPPE: Formerly Bell's, supplying rope for gallows in Grassmarket. Now antiques and bric-à-brac
WEST BOW NEEDLE ART: tapestry & embroidery
Antiques: lots of prints, needlework kits
SCORE COMMOTIONS: jokes inc. bottled knickes
BOW-WELL ANTIQUES
ARCH LEATHER Co.: bags and jackets
PRIVATE LINES: underwear and lingerie
LAST DROP: pub food: opposite the old gallows
PARTNERS: fussy fashion, some designer labels
SHEEPISH LOOKS: Bill Baber
GENNARO: pizzeria, reasonable prices
SWING: funky cothes and hip tented ceiling
PIERRE VICTOIRE: newest of three P.V. restaurants
WHITE HART INN
MAMMAS: pizzas
BEEHIVE INN: a la carte meals. Drones Bar - real ale and good pub food
BLACK BULL
IMAGES OF NEPAL: earrings, puppets and cards of Edinburgh (not Nepal)!
ERIC DAVIDSON
HELIOS FOUNTAIN: crafts: books, toys, beads and kits. Veggie café - biodynamically and organically grown ingredients

George IV Bridge
Cowgate

PRESERVATION HALL: live music and bar lunches
TRADER VIC'S: wine bar
BYZANTIUM
A huge pot-pourri of stalls on three floors.
- many antique/junk stalls, Moroccan jewellery and clothes. Classical music.
BALI-HI: Indonesian earrings, carvings, clothes, bags
KALEIDOS: kites that fly.
ILLUMINI: stained glass, ceramics.
IN STITCHES: cushions and clothes
RUDRA: Indian bedspreads, scarves
TERRACOTTA: bags, rugs, Kilims from central Turkey Upstairs: changing contemporary art for sale and more antique stalls.
CAFÉ: good coffee in pots - choice of blend. Also salads, cakes and hot specials

Street
Steps
Victoria
West Bow

ST ELMO'S: bar with US diner food
LONG TALL SALLY: stylish clothes for tall women
BOW BAR (W Frazer - spirit merchant) pies and other food
ROUND THE WORLD: ethnic/designer gadgets
KINNELLS: café - sandwiches etc
KINNELLS: freshly ground coffee, jams, deli
EYE CATCHERS: size 14+ womens clothes
LOCO: cards and gifts
WEST BOW ANTIQUES
SCOT ROCKS

Candlemaker Row

TRAVERSE THEATRE: through alleyway and tunnels. Bar open until after performances. Food 11-7. Art for sale
SERENDIPITY: antiques, clothes and bric-à-brac
WIND THINGS: kites, frisbees, boomerangs, and parachuting teddy bears

MR WOOD'S FOSSILS: take home a piece of ancient Scotland
CANDLEMAKERS ARMS

J7
J8
H7
H8

MULHERRON ANTIQUES

Hunter's Close

Grassmarket
Heriot Bridge

N

TRADERS FOR MEN: jeans, jackets and other menswear
MAY MALLINSON ANTIQUES: hats, wood shafted golf clubs, jelly pans, bibles etc
THE GRASSMARKET: antiques

G7 H7

FIDDLERS ARMS
SIMPLY SHETLAND: jumpers

H8
G8

Victoria Street and Grassmarket

0   50   100
Yards

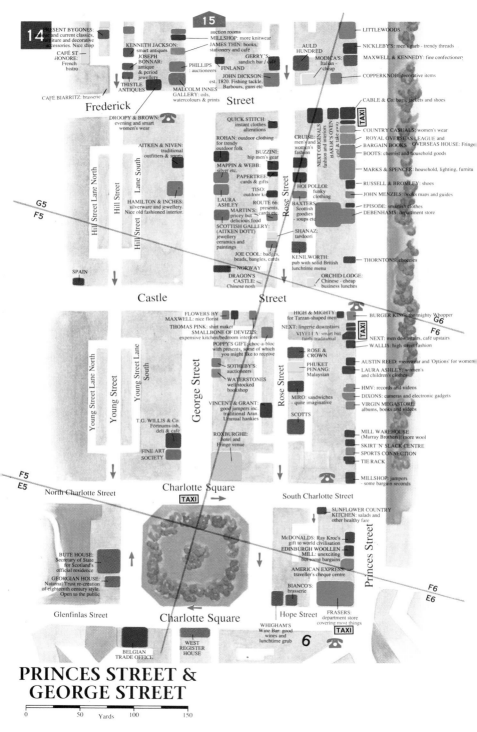

PRINCES STREET & GEORGE STREET

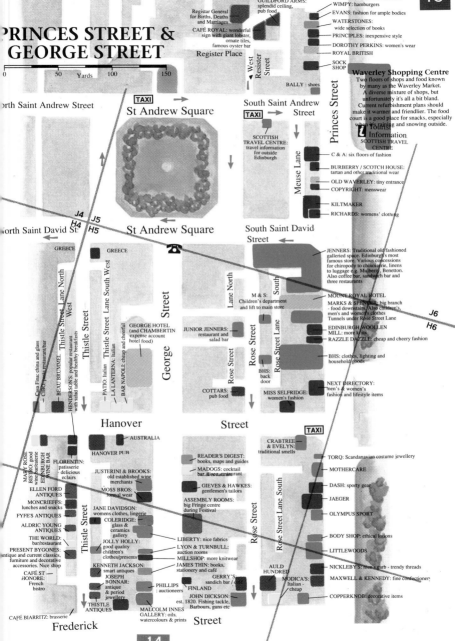

PRINCES STREET & GEORGE STREET

SCOTTISH RECORD OFFICE

WIMPY: hamburgers

EVANS: fashion for ample bodies

WATERSTONES: wide selection of books

PRINCIPLES: inexpensive style

DOROTHY PERKINS: women's wear

ROYAL BRITISH

SOCK SHOP

GUILDFORD ARMS: splendid ceiling, pub food

Registar General for Births, Deaths and Marriages

CAFÉ ROYAL: wonderful sign with giant lobster, ornate tiles, famous oyster bar

Register Place

Princes Street

BALLY : shoes

Waverley Shopping Centre
Two floors of shops and food known by many as the Waverley Market. A diverse mixture of shops, but unfortunately it's all a bit bland. Current refurbishment plans should make it warmer and friendlier. The food court is a good place for snacks, especially when it's raining and snowing outside.

i Information

SCOTTISH TRAVEL CENTRE

C & A: six floors of fashion

BURBERRY / SCOTCH HOUSE: tartan and other traditional wear

OLD WAVERLEY: tiny entrance

COPYRIGHT: menswear

KILTMAKER

RICHARDS: womens' clothing

0   50   Yards   100   150

orth Saint Andrew Street

TAXI

St Andrew Square

South Saint Andrew Street

TAXI

SCOTTISH TRAVEL CENTRE: travel information for outside Edinburgh

West Resister Street

Meuse Lane

J4 J5
H4 H5

orth Saint David St.

St Andrew Square

South Saint David Street

JENNERS: Traditional old fashioned galleried space. Edinburgh's most famous store. Various concessions for chiropody to chinoiserie, linens to luggage e.g. Mulberry, Benetton. Also coffee bar, sandwich bar and three restaurants

GREECE

GREECE

☎

M & S: Children's department and lift to main store

MOUNT ROYAL HOTEL

MARKS & SPENCER: big branch - food downstairs. Also children's, men's and women's clothes. Tunnels under Rose Street Lane

J6
H6

EDINBURGH WOOLLEN MILL: more knits

RAZZLE DAZZLE: cheap and cheery fashion

BHS: clothes, lighting and household goods

BHS: back door

NEXT DIRECTORY: men's & women's fashion and lifestyle items

GEORGE HOTEL (and CHAMBERTIN expense account hotel food)

Casa Fina: china and glass

CIBO: pasta restaurant/bar

BEAU BRUMMEL

Thistle Street Lane North West

Thistle Street Lane North

Thistle Street

Thistle Street Lane South West

PATIO: Italian

LA LANTERNA: Italian

BAR NAPOLI: cheap and cheerful

HENDERSONS: popular restaurant with salad table and healthy breakfasts

George Street

Lane North

Rose Street

South

Rose Street Lane

JUNIOR JENNERS: restaurant and salad bar

Rose Street

COTTARS: pub food

BHS: back door

MISS SELFRIDGE: women's fashion

Hanover Street

Street

TAXI

AUSTRALIA

HANOVER PUB

MARY ROSE BISTRO: good wine bar/eaterie

EDINBURGH WINE BAR

FLORENTIN: patisserie - delicious eclairs

ELLEN FORD ANTIQUES

MONCRIEFFS: lunches and snacks

FYFE'S ANTIQUES

ALDRIC YOUNG ANTIQUES

THE WORLD: bar/restaurant

PRESENT BYGONES: antique and current classics, furniture and decorative accessories. Nice shop

CAFÉ ST HONORE: French bistro

JUSTERINI & BROOKS: old established wine merchants

MOSS BROS: formal wear

JANE DAVIDSON: womens clothes, lingerie

COLERIDGE: glass & ceramics gallery

JOLLY HOLLY: good quality children's clothes/presents

KENNETH JACKSON: smart antiques

JOSEPH BONNAR: antique & period jewellery

Thistle Street

THISTLE ANTIQUES

READER'S DIGEST: books, maps and guides

MADOGS: cocktail bar & restaurant

GIEVES & HAWKES: gentlemen's tailors

ASSEMBLY ROOMS: big Fringe centre during Festival

LIBERTY: nice fabrics

LYON & TURNBULL: auction rooms

MILLSHOP: more knitwear

JAMES THIN: books, stationery and café

GERRY'S: sandich bar / café

PHILLIPS : auctioneers

FINLAND

JOHN DICKSON est. 1820. Fishing tackle, Barbours, guns etc

MALCOLM INNES GALLERY: oils, watercolours & prints

CRABTREE & EVELYN: traditional smells

Rose Street

Rose Street Lane South

AULD HUNDRED

MODICA'S: Italian - cheap

TAXI

TORQ: Scandanavian costume jewellery

MOTHERCARE

DASH: sporty gear

JAEGER

OLYMPUS SPORT

BODY SHOP: ethical lotions

LITTLEWOODS

NICKLEBY'S: men's garb - trendy threads

MAXWELL & KENNEDY: fine confectionery

COPPERKNOB: decorative items

Frederick   Street

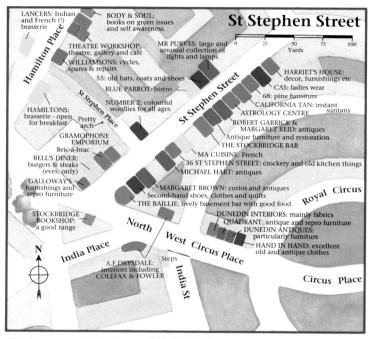

LANCERS: Indian and French (!) brasserie

BODY & SOUL: books on green issues and self awareness

St Stephen Street

THEATRE WORKSHOP: theatre, gallery and café

MR PURVES: large and unusual collection of lights and lamps

0   25   50   75   100
Yards

WILLIAMSONS: cycles, spares & repairs

55: old hats, coats and shoes

HARRIET'S HOUSE: decor, furnishings etc

BLUE PARROT: bistro

St Stephen Street

CAS: ladies wear

68: pine furniture

NUMBER 2: colourful woollies for all ages

CALIFORNIA TAN: instant suntans

ASTROLOGY CENTRE

HAMILTONS: brasserie - open for breakfast

Pretty arch

St Stephen Place

ROBERT GARRICK & MARGARET REID: antiques

GRAMOPHONE EMPORIUM

Antique furniture and restoration

THE STOCKBRIDGE BAR

Bric-à-brac

MA CUISINE: French

BELL'S DINER: burgers & steaks (eves. only)

36 ST STEPHEN STREET: crockery and old kitchen things

MICHAEL HART: antiques

GALLOWAY'S furnishings and repro furniture

MARGARET BROWN: curios and antiques

Second-hand shoes, clothes and quilts

Royal   Circus

THE BAILLIE: lively basement bar with good food

STOCKBRIDGE BOOKSHOP: a good range

DUNEDIN INTERIORS: mainly fabrics

QUADRANT: antique and repro furniture

North

DUNEDIN ANTIQUES: particularly furniture

West   Circus   Place

HAND IN HAND: excellent old and antique clothes

N

India Place

Steps

A.F. DRYSDALE: interiors including COLEFAX & FOWLER

India St

Circus   Place

The above area can be found on page 24 (grid ref. F3)

Waverley Shopping Centre

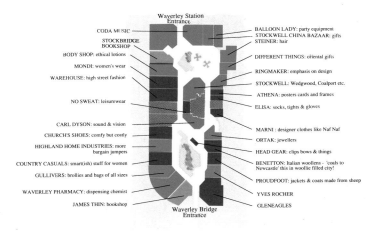

Waverley Station Entrance

CODA MUSIC
STOCKBRIDGE BOOKSHOP
BODY SHOP: ethical lotions
MONDI: women's wear
WAREHOUSE: high street fashion
NO SWEAT: leisurewear
CARL DYSON: sound & vision
CHURCH'S SHOES: comfy but costly
HIGHLAND HOME INDUSTRIES: more bargain jumpers
COUNTRY CASUALS: smart(ish) stuff for women
GULLIVERS: brollies and bags of all sizes
WAVERLEY PHARMACY: dispensing chemist
JAMES THIN: bookshop

BALLOON LADY: party equipment
STOCKWELL CHINA BAZAAR: gifts
STEINER: hair
DIFFERENT THINGS: oriental gifts
RINGMAKER: emphasis on design
STOCKWELL: Wedgwood, Coalport etc.
ATHENA: posters cards and frames
ELISA: socks, tights & gloves
MARNI : designer clothes like Naf Naf
ORTAK: jewellers
HEAD GEAR: clips bows & things
BENETTON: Italian woollens - 'coals to Newcastle' this in woollie filled city!
PROUDFOOT: jackets & coats made from sheep
YVES ROCHER
GLENEAGLES

Waverley Bridge Entrance

UPPER LEVEL

Situated at the east end of Princes Street.
See J5, both on the main map (page 35)
and on the Princes Street map (page 15)

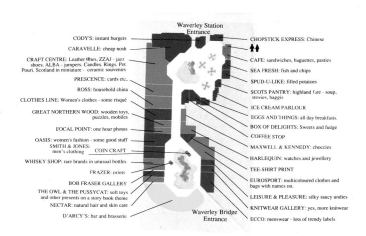

Waverley Station Entrance

CODY'S: instant burgers
CARAVELLE: cheap nosh
CRAFT CENTRE: Leather lines, ZZAJ - jazz shoes. ALBA - jumpers. Candles. Rings. Pot Pouri. Scotland in miniature - ceramic souvenirs
PRESCENCE: cards etc.
ROSS: household china
CLOTHES LINE: Women's clothes - some risqué
GREAT NORTHERN WOOD: wooden toys, puzzles, mobiles
FOCAL POINT: one hour photos
OASIS: women's fashion - some good stuff
SMITH & JONES: men's clothing   COIN CRAFT
WHISKY SHOP: rare brands in unusual bottles
FRAZER: prints
BOB FRASER GALLERY
THE OWL & THE PUSSYCAT: soft toys and other presents on a story book theme
NECTAR: natural hair and skin care
D'ARCY'S: bar and brasserie

CHOPSTICK EXPRESS: Chinese
CAFE: sandwiches, baguettes, pasties
SEA FRESH: fish and chips
SPUD-U-LIKE: filled potatoes
SCOTS PANTRY: highland fare - soup, stovies, haggis
ICE CREAM PARLOUR
EGGS AND THINGS: all day breakfasts.
BOX OF DELIGHTS: Sweets and fudge
COFFEE STOP
MAXWELL & KENNEDY: choccies
HARLEQUIN: watches and jewellery
TEE-SHIRT PRINT
EUROSPORT: multicoloured clothes and bags with names on.
LEISURE & PLEASURE: silky saucy undies
KNITWEAR GALLERY: yes, more knitwear
ECCO: menswear - lots of trendy labels

Waverley Bridge Entrance

LOWER LEVEL

ROYAL BOTANIC GARDEN

0   50   100   150   200
Yards

Inverleith Place

Alpine Houses

Palm Houses

PALM HOUSE

Demonstration Garden

Copse

Rhododendron Walk

Exhibition & Visitors' Centre

Terrace Café
Sit outside in summer. Daily specials - hot & cold dishes

Inverleith House
Georgian mansion housing temporary exhibitions

City View Point
looking south south east to Castle and city spires

WEST GATE

West Lodge

Arboretum

Arboretum Road

Inverleith

GARDENS

Demonstration Garden
Lots of handy tips and
suggestions for gardeners.

Copse
Magnolias, lilies,
Rhododrendrons,
hollies and other
native species.

Azalea Lawn
Beautiful colours in May.

Rhododrendron Walk
A riot of colour in June.

Pond
Many lilies and water-loving plants.
Also Gunnera manicata - leaves over
one metre across.

Heath Garden
Over 30 varieties of heather.

Peat Garden
Constructed in 1939. Demand for peat
from gardeners has meant that peat
supplies are now under threat. The
light damp soil supports lilies, orchids
and dwarf/creeping shrubs, including
many Auastralasian species.

Rock Garden
All sorts of creeping conifers,
cotoneasters alpine and other shrubs,
including some from New Zealand.

Arboretum
Deciduous and conifer, fruit bearing
and flowering. Most beautiful in
autumn. See the unusual white-barked
birch trees.

Woodland Garden
American Sequoias (though somewhat
stunted), other conifers and
Rhododrendrons.

EXHIBITION PLANT HOUSES

Hire a 'soundalive' 40 minute tour on tape.
Things to look out for:

Temperate House
Plants which find Scotland a bit chilly.

Cactus & Succulent House
Shows how American and African plants
adapted in the same ways to similar conditions
though very far apart.

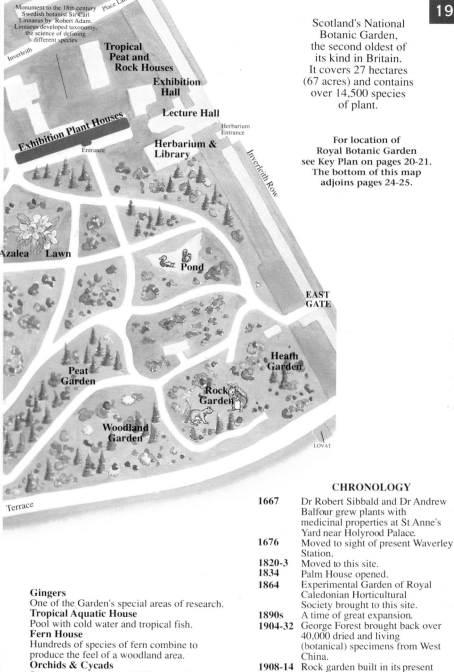

Monument to the 18th century Swedish botanist Sir Carl Linnaeus by Robert Adam. Linnaeus developed taxonomy, the science of defining different species

Place Lane

Inverleith

Tropical Peat and Rock Houses

Exhibition Hall

Exhibition Plant Houses

Lecture Hall

Entrance

Herbarium Entrance

Herbarium & Library

Inverleith Row

Azalea Lawn

Pond

EAST GATE

Heath Garden

Peat Garden

Rock Garden

LOVAT

Woodland Garden

Terrace

Scotland's National Botanic Garden, the second oldest of its kind in Britain. It covers 27 hectares (67 acres) and contains over 14,500 species of plant.

For location of **Royal Botanic Garden** see Key Plan on pages 20-21. The bottom of this map adjoins pages 24-25.

CHRONOLOGY

1667	Dr Robert Sibbald and Dr Andrew Balfour grew plants with medicinal properties at St Anne's Yard near Holyrood Palace.
1676	Moved to sight of present Waverley Station.
1820-3	Moved to this site.
1834	Palm House opened.
1864	Experimental Garden of Royal Caledonian Horticultural Society brought to this site.
1890s	A time of great expansion.
1904-32	George Forest brought back over 40,000 dried and living (botanical) specimens from West China.
1908-14	Rock garden built in its present form.
1980	Voted best garden in Europe.

Gingers
One of the Garden's special areas of research.
Tropical Aquatic House
Pool with cold water and tropical fish.
Fern House
Hundreds of species of fern combine to produce the feel of a woodland area.
Orchids & Cycads
Some cycads are around 200 years old.
Citrus & Tea plants

EDINBURGH KEY PLAN

SCALE

```
0    0.25   0.5   0.75   1              KILOMETRES
0          0.5           1         1.5        2   MILE
```

Finding your way around the atlas

This plan shows the relative positions of each page and of different parts of the city. The relationship of these areas to the city outskirts, surrounding countryside and local places of interest is shown on the *Around Edinburgh* map (pages 62-63).

➤ The red arrows on pages 22 to 53 will lead you from section to section.

The relative positions of pages are also shown at the bottom of each right-hand page.

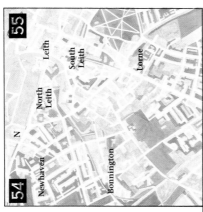

Points of Reference

- A BR Waverley Station
- B Bus Station (St Andrew Square)
- C Calton Hill
- D Camera Obscura
- E Canongate Tolbooth
- F Dean Bridge
- G Edinburgh Castle
- H Edinburgh University

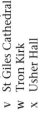

J   Greyfriars Bobby and
    Greyfriars Kirk
K   Holyroodhouse
L   Holyrood Park
M   King's Theatre
N   Leith Docks
P   National Gallery and
    Royal Scottish Academy
Q   Museum of Scotland
R   National Gallery
    of Modern Art
S   National Portrait Gallery
T   Playhouse Theatre
U   Royal Infirmary
V   St Giles Cathedral
W   Tron Kirk
X   Usher Hall

Expanded maps and plans

Page

7   **Edinburgh Castle:** perched on a mound of volcanic granite; steeped in history and dominating the city around it.

8-11   **Royal Mile:** the historic route from the Castle to the Palace of Hoyroodhouse. Home to endless chilling, often apocryphal, stories.

13   **Victoria Street and Grassmarket:** a large collection of interesting shops and more pubs than are good for you.

14-15   **Princes Street and George Street:** famous shopping streets and the city's financial centre.

16   **St Stephen's Street, Stockbridge:** hunting ground for clothes, antiques and bric-à-brac.

17   **Waverley Shopping Centre:** food court and dozens of fashion and theme shops.

18-19   **Royal Botanic Garden:** splendid, historic collection within walking distance of the centre.

A　　　　　　　　　　　　　　　**B**

Built with a trust of more than half a
million pounds stemming from the
estate of William Fettes, grocer, military stores
contractor, underwriter and tea/coffee merchant,
who died in 1836

**FETTES
COLLEGE**

East

1

More like a French château
than a school (from the outside).
James Bond was supposed to
have been a pupil here

Road

Carrington

Impressive set of gates

Road

Carrington

School

Fettes

19/39 28/29
41A 82A 83
81/81A/81B

Police rugby ground

C1 C2 X64 65
X65 129/X29

Avenue

Playing Fields

2

Crewe

POLICE HEADQUARTERS

Road

Comely B

Comely
Bank
Cemetery

South

Comely

Big SAFEWAY
Supermarket

Comely

Learmonth

C1 C2 X64 65

19/39 20 28/29
80 81/81A
81B 82A 83

Learmonth
Park

Learmon

UNUSUAL GATE HOUSE
One of the entrances to the
ROYAL VICTORIA
HOSPITAL.

X65 129 X129

80

School

Crescent

3

Craigleith Road

Orchard

Road

Orchard

Brae

Comely

Orchard

Orchard
Grove

armonth

Avenue

Comely

| Cafés/Snacks | Pubs | Restaurants | Hotels | Cinemas | Theatres |

This part of Edinburgh was developed in the early nineteenth century.
An early resident was Thomas Carlyle who moved to 21 Comely Bank in May 1826. He worked on his
writing, while treating visitors as "nauseous intruders" and eating mutton chops at four in the afternoon.

From the steps at the end of South Learmonth Avenue (B4 on page 30), there is a good view of Fettes.
The area to the north of Comely Bank used to be the estate of Sir William Fettes (see note beside school).

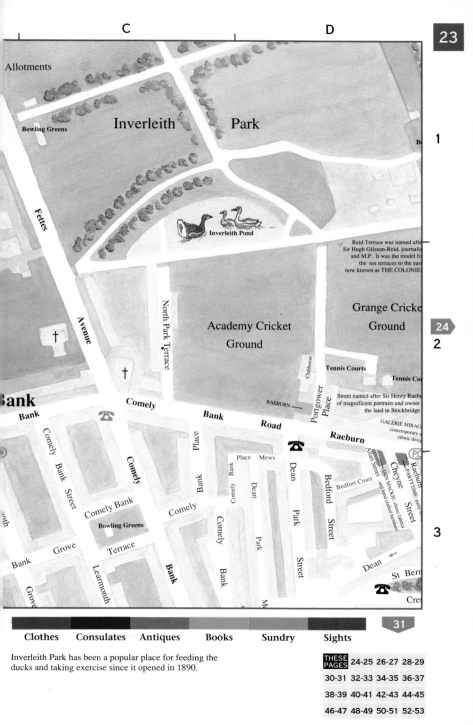

Inverleith   Park

Inverleith Pond

Reid Terrace was named afte[r]
Sir Hugh Gilzean-Reid, journalis[t]
and M.P.. It was the model fo[r]
the ten terraces to the eas[t]
now known as THE COLONIE[S]

Bank

North Park Terrace

Fettes

Avenue

Academy Cricket
Ground

Grange Crick[et]
Ground

Clubhouse

Tennis Courts

Tennis Cou[rts]

RAEBURN

Portgower Place

Street named after Sir Henry Raebu[rn]
of magnificent portraits and owner
the land in Stockbridge

Comely

Bank   Road

Raeburn

GALERIE MIRAG[E]
contemporary a[nd]
ethnic desig[n]

Comely Bank Street

Comely

Place

Place   Mews

Comely Bank

Dean

Bedford Court

Allan Street

Cheyne

Raeburn

PARTYTIME party [...]
IAN MACKIE: flint fabrics
and hand crafted furniture

PC

Comely Bank

Bowling Greens

Comely

Dean

Bedford

Street

Comely

Grove

Terrace

Comely

Park

Street

Bank

Dean

St Ber[nard's]

Bank

Grove

Learmonth

Bank

Street

Cres[cent]

| Clothes | Consulates | Antiques | Books | Sundry | Sights |

Inverleith Park has been a popular place for feeding the
ducks and taking exercise since it opened in 1890.

1

2

3

D

THESE PAGES 24-25 26-27 28-29
30-31 32-33 34-35 36-37
38-39 40-41 42-43 44-45
46-47 48-49 50-51 52-53

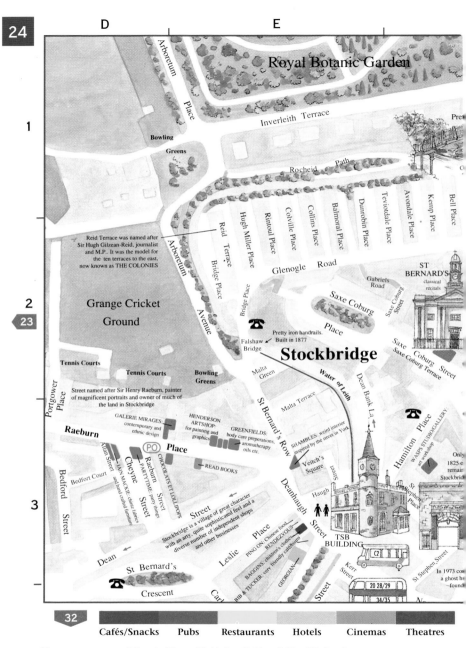

D

E

Arboretum Place

Royal Botanic Garden

Pre

1

Inverleith Terrace

Bowling

Greens

Rocheid Path

G

Reid Terrace

Hugh Miller Place

Rintoul Place

Colville Place

Collins Place

Balmoral Place

Dunrobin Place

Teviotdale Place

Avondale Place

Kemp Place

Bell Place

Reid Terrace was named after
Sir Hugh Gilzean-Reid, journalist
and M.P.. It was the model for
the ten terraces to the east,
now known as THE COLONIES

Arboretum

Glenogle Road

ST BERNARD'S
classical
recitals

Gabriels
Road

Bridge Place

Saxe Coburg

Place

Saxe Coburg Street

2

23

Grange Cricket Ground

Arboretum Avenue

☎

Pretty iron handrails.
Built in 1877

Falshaw
Bridge

Stockbridge

Saxe Coburg Street

Saxe Coburg Terrace

Tennis Courts

Tennis Courts

Bowling Greens

Street named after Sir Henry Raeburn, painter
of magnificent portraits and owner of much of
the land in Stockbridge

Malta Green

Water of Leith

Dean Bank La.

Portgower Place

GALERIE MIRAGES:
contemporary and
ethnic design

HENDERSON
ARTSHOP-
for painting and
graphics

GREENFIELDS:
body care preparations,
aromatherapy
oils etc.

St Bernard's Row

Malta Terrace

SHAMBLES: weird interior
inspired by the street in York.

☎

W ASPS STUDIO GALLERY:
art workshop

Hamilton Place

Raeburn

Allan Street

Bedford Street

Bedford Court

Cheyne

Street

IAIN MACKIE: china/ fabric
and hand crafted furniture

PO

CHOCOLATS ET LOLLIPOPS

Raeburn Street

PARTYTIME: party things

Place

READ BOOKS

Veitch's
Square

Only
1825 e
remain
Stockbrid

St Stephen Place

3

Street

Stockbridge is a village of great character
with an arty, quite sophisticated feel and a
diverse number of independent shops
and other businesses

Deanhaugh Street

Haugh Street

☎

Dean

St Bernard's

Crescent

Leslie Place

PING ON: Chinese food

RENDEZVOUS

BAGGINS: children's clothes

BIB & TUCKER: very friendly cafe/shop

GEORGIAN

Cat

Street

TSB BUILDING

C2

Kerr Street

St Stephen Street

In 1973 co
a ghost h
found

20 28/29

34/35

N

32

Cafés/Snacks   Pubs   Restaurants   Hotels   Cinemas   Theatres

There are two ways to follow the Water of Leith from Falshaw Bridge (E2 above).
Either follow the north side along Arboretum Avenue or walk along Glenogle Road
past 'the Colonies', left beside Bell Place and over the footbridge to rejoin Rocheid Path.

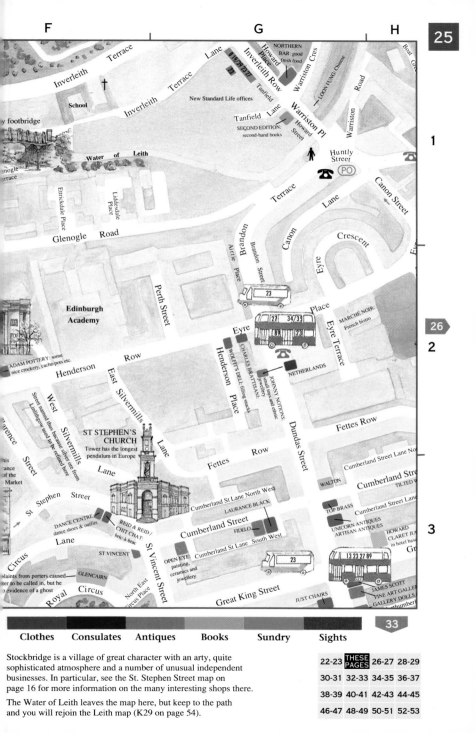

Clothes Consulates Antiques Books Sundry Sights

Stockbridge is a village of great character with an arty, quite sophisticated atmosphere and a number of unusual independent businesses. In particular, see the St. Stephen Street map on page 16 for more information on the many interesting shops there.

The Water of Leith leaves the map here, but keep to the path and you will rejoin the Leith map (K29 on page 54).

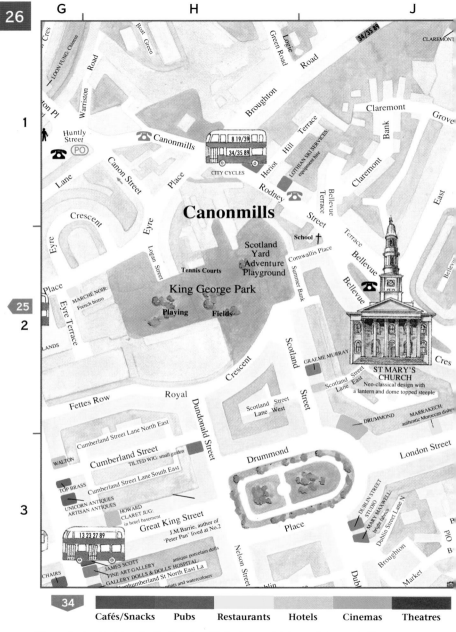

1

25

2

3

34

Cafés/Snacks Pubs Restaurants Hotels Cinemas Theatres

You used to be able to buy food in Broughton Market but now it is just workshops and offices.

K — See Leith map on page 54 — L

Cres
Street
West Annandale Street
Bellevue Gardens
Bellevue Street
Bellevue Street
McDonald Place
McDonald McDonald Street
McDonald Road
Dryden Terr

Annandale Street
Road

1

Bellevue Gro

Hopetoun Street

Bellevue Street

und Terrace

Street

Green

Hopetoun Cres

Broughton

(York Place 300 yards south of here)
No.10: home of George Watson, founder of the Royal Scottish Academy

No.40: home of Alexander Osborne, Commissioner of Customs and the tallest man in Edinburgh of his day (early 19th century). "His legs were nearly as large as the body of an ordinary person". He used to eat 9 pounds of steak at a sitting

Bellevue Place

Annandale

Hopetoun Street

Hopetoun Cres La

What should have been a beautiful crescent never finished and became dominated by surrounding light industry

28

2

Mansfield Place

School
Cochran Terrace

ST ANDREW'S HALL
Fringe venue
☎ 8 13 19/39

East

School
Shaw Square

London
Street

Gayfield Square

Gayfield Place Lane

Gayfield Place Lane

Street

Street

Ann

C3 C16

Broughton Place

Place
Lane

†

Union Street
Gayfield Street

Gayfield Square

Gayfield
Haddington

Gayfield Place

BLUE MOON CAFÉ:
time food & gallery
Fringe venue

PO

The basement of 46 Broughton Street was the local Tolbooth dungeon

MRS BEETON'S:
deli with snacks
EDINBURGH CENTRE: sandwiches
DRACAEUS

New Broughton

Broughton Place

Broughton Place

Barony Place

PHILLIPINE ISLAND: south seas bistro/take-out

BARONY BAR:
friendly place

TENACIOUS HIDE:
smart slinky leather clothes

Broughton

Hart Street

EDINBURGH PRINTMAKERS WORKSHOP GALLERY

South Gayfield Lane

POLICE

Elm Row
VALVONA & C
good deli and

3

ghton Place
Albany Street
KHUSHI: Indian nosh

Street
Lane

bany
Lane

Forth Street

Union Street

RADIO FORTH

PIERRE VICTOIRE: simple decor, good French food

VICTO

Lane

S's PEARL

Antigua Street

Walk

Blenheim Place

35

| Clothes | Consulates | Antiques | Books | Sundry | Sights |

This was the old Barony of Broughton. Broughton Street offers a good selection of places to eat and drink.

The top edge of this page adjoins the Leith map on page 54.

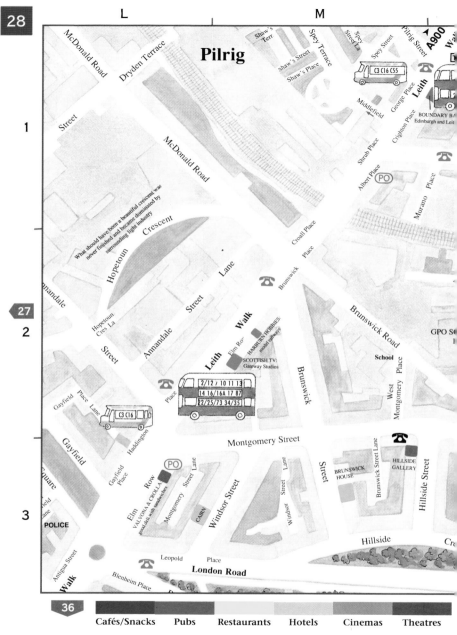

Pilrig

Thomas Carlyle lived in Pilrig (Spey Street) in 1822-4 , and a howling dog gave him
many sleepless nights. Around this time he recorded that he was charged
"the unreasonable sum" of 15/2d (76p) for a full week's board and lodging.

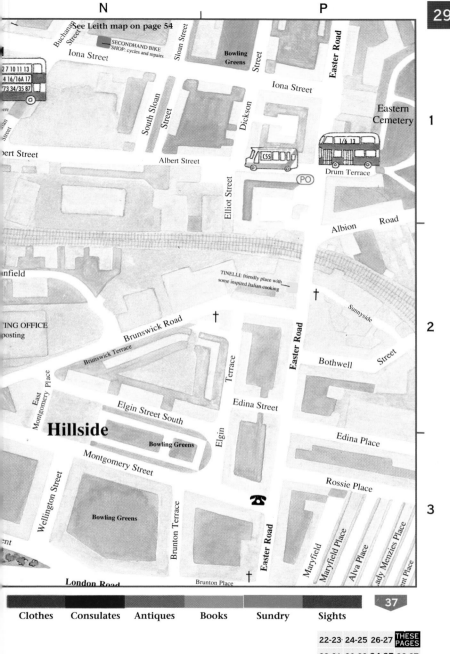

N

P

See Leith map on page 54

Buchanan Street

SECONDHAND BIKE SHOP: cycles and repairs

Iona Street

Sloan Street

Bowling Greens

Easter Road

27 10 11 13
4 16/16A 17
73 34/35 87

Iona Street

South Sloan Street

Dickson Street

Eastern Cemetery

1

ert Street

Albert Street

Elliot Street

C55

1/6 13

Drum Terrace

PO

Albion Road

nfield

TINELLI: friendly place with some inspired Italian cooking

Sunnyside

†

2

TING OFFICE posting

Brunswick Road

Brunswick Terrace

†

Terrace

Easter Road

Bothwell

Street

East Montgomery Place

Elgin Street South

Edina Street

Edina Place

Hillside

Bowling Greens

Elgin

Wellington Street

Montgomery Street

Brunton Terrace

☎

Rossie Place

3

Bowling Greens

Easter Road

Maryfield

Maryfield Place

Alva Place

dy Menzies Place

n Place

ent

London Road

Brunton Place

†

Clothes	Consulates	Antiques	Books	Sundry	Sights

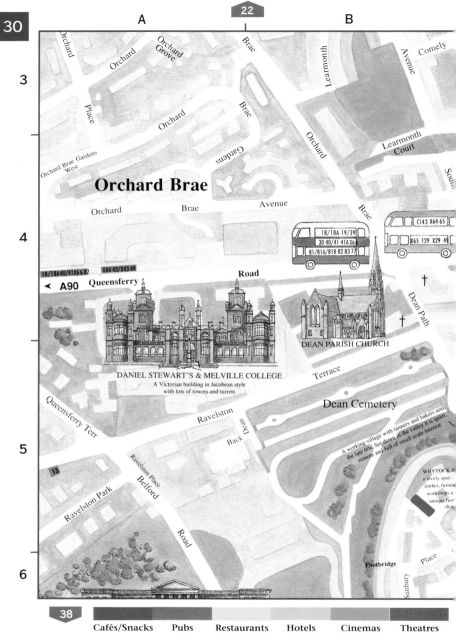

A 22 B

3

Orchard Brae

4

← A90 Queensferry   Road

18/18A 19/39
30 40/41 41A X6
81/81A/81B 82 83 77

CI43 X64 65

X65 129 X29 49

DANIEL STEWART'S & MELVILLE COLLEGE
A Victorian building in Jacobean style
with lots of towers and turrets

DEAN PARISH CHURCH

Terrace

Dean Cemetery

A working village with tanners and bakers until
the late 60s. Set down in the valley it is quiet,
remote and full of small-scale interest

WHYTOCK &
a lovely spot -
timber, furnit
workshops a
antique furn
shop

5

Ravelston

13

Ravelston Place

Belford

Ravelston Park

Road

6

Footbridge

Place

Cafés/Snacks   Pubs   Restaurants   Hotels   Cinemas   Theatres

Dean Cemetery is very peaceful and full of splendid trees and plants in between grandiose Victorian mausoleums. Dean Village was a working village with tanners and bakers until the late 1960s. Set down in the valley it is quiet, remote and full of small-scale interest.

During the twelfth century St. Bernard of Clairvaux is believed by some to have sheltered in a cave near Dean Bridge. Local spring water was said to have helped him recover from illness and carry on his mission, raising support for the Second Crusade. It is, however, unlikely that St Bernard ever came to Scotland.

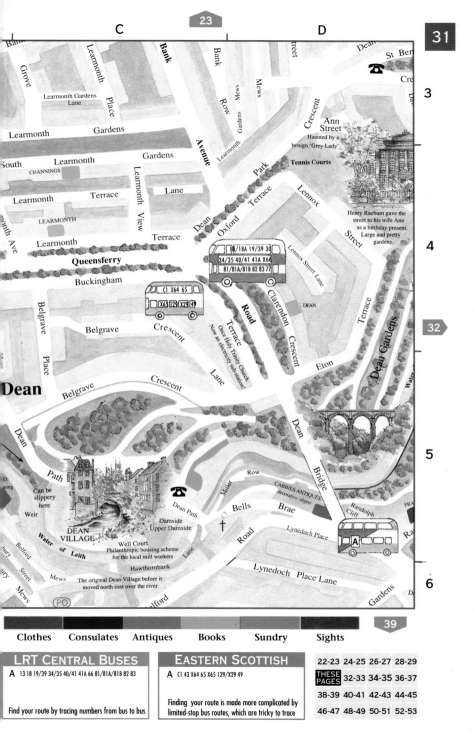

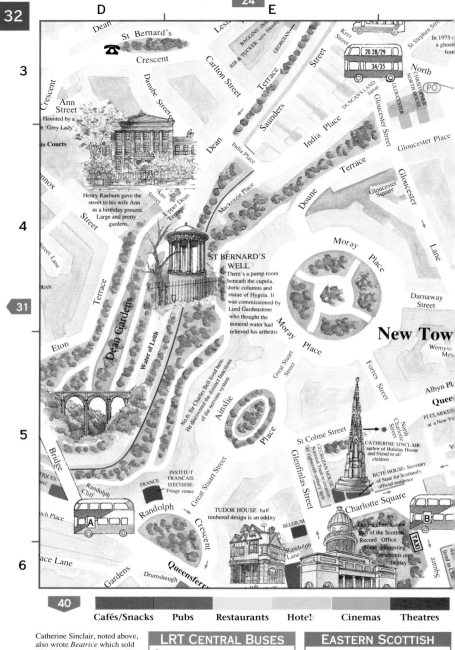

3

D   E

Dean

St Bernard's

☎

Crescent

Leslie

BAGGINS: child-
BIB & TUCKER: very friendly

GEORGIAN

Street

Kerr
Street

St Stephen Stre

In 1973
a ghost
fou

20 28/29

34/35

North

Crescent

Ann
Street

Haunted by a
'Grey Lady'

Danube Street

Carlton Street

Saunders

Terrace

DUNCAN'S LAND:
Italian

Gloucester Street

CHRISTOPHER
NORTH HOUSE

PO

Street

Dean

India Place

India Place

Gloucester

Place

Gloucester

is Courts

Terrace

GLOUCESTER

ennox

Ann
Street

Upper Dean

Terrace

Mackenzie Place

Doune

Terrace

Gloucester
Square

Gloucester

Lane

Henry Raeburn gave the
street to his wife Ann
as a birthday present.
Large and pretty
gardens.

4

Street

Street Lane

DEAN

Terrace

Eton

ST BERNARD'S
WELL
There's a pump room
beneath the cupola,
doric columns and
statue of Hygeia. It
was commissioned by
Lord Gardenstone
who thought the
mineral water had
relieved his arthritis

Moray

Place

Darnaway
Street

31

Dean Gardens

Water of Leith

No.6: Sir Charles Bell lived here.
He discovered the distinct functions
of the nervous system

Moray

Place

Great Stuart
Street

Moray

Place

Forres Street

New Tow

Wemyss
Mev

Albyn Pl

Quee

Ainslie

Place

PJ CLARKES
at a New Ye

Bridge

och Place

Randolph
Cliff

A

INSTITUT
FRANÇAIS
D'ECOSSE:
Fringe venue

FRANCE

Randolph

Crescent

Great Stuart Street

St Colme Street

Glenfinlas Street

North
Charlotte
Street

CATHERINE SINCLAIR:
author of Holiday House
and friend to all
children

GEORGIAN HOUSE:
National Trust re-creation
of eighteenth century style

BUTE HOUSE: Secretary
of State for Scotland's
official residence

Charlotte Square

B

TAXI

TUDOR HOUSE: half
timbered design is an oddity

BELGIUM

Once a church, now
part of the Scottish
Record Office.
Some interesting
documents on
display

A
lived in Cha

Sum

5

6

ace Lane

Gardens

Queensferr

Drumsheugh

Randolph
Lane

40

Cafés/Snacks   Pubs   Restaurants   Hotels   Cinemas   Theatres

Catherine Sinclair, noted above,
also wrote *Beatrice* which sold
100,000 copies in America. She
opened cooking depôts where the
poor could get a good meal for
2-4p, and built Edinburgh's first
public fountain and a number of
cabmen's shelters in the city.

LRT Central Buses

A 13 18 19/39 34/35 40/41 41A 66 81/81A/81B 82 83

B 13 18 19/39 34/35 40/41 41A 81/81A/81B 82 83

Find your route by tracing numbers from bus to bus

Eastern Scottish

A C1 43 X64 65 X65 129/X29 49

B C1 43 X64 65 X65 129/X29 49

C C1 EX1 EX2 EX3 EX4 C2 X08 16 17 18 X21 X22 X24 X26
27 X29/129 X32 X33 X34 37 43 X43 45 49 72
X77 79 X79 X82 X84 273 274 276 281 X64 X65

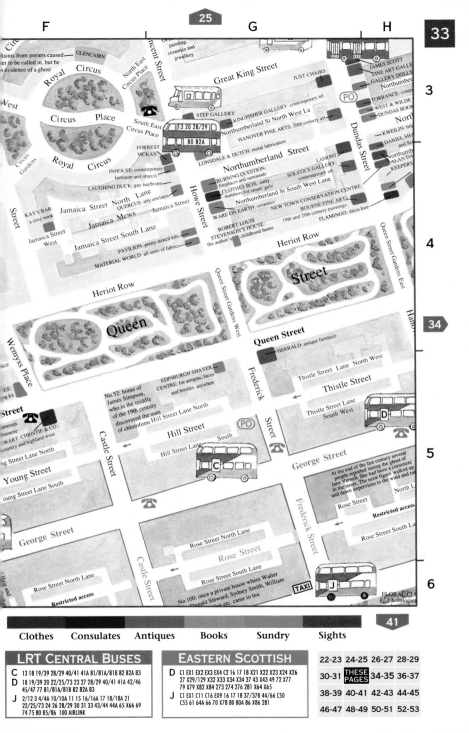

Clothes   Consulates   Antiques   Books   Sundry   Sights

LRT CENTRAL BUSES

C 13 18 19/39 28/29 40/41 41A 81/81A/81B 82 82A 83

D 18 19/39 20 22/25/73 23 27 28/29 40/41 41A 42/46 45/47 77 81/81A/81B 82 82A 83

J 2/12 3 4/4A 10/10A 11 15 16/16A 17 18/18A 21 22/25/73 24 26 28/29 30 31 33 43/44 44A 65 X66 69 74 75 80 85/86 100 AIRLINK

EASTERN SCOTTISH

D C1 EX1 EX2 EX3 EX4 C2 16 17 18 X21 X22 X23 X24 X26 27 X29/129 X32 X33 X34 X34 37 43 X43 49 72 X77 79 X79 X82 X84 273 274 276 281 X64 X65

J C1 EX1 C11 C16 EX9 16 17 18 37/37B 44/66 C50 C55 61 64A 66 70 X78 80 80A 86 X86 281

41

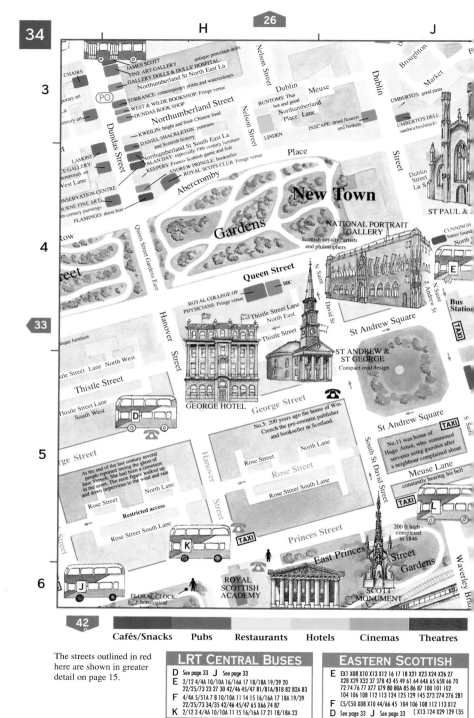

H | **J**

3

JAMES SCOTT: antique porcelain dolls
FINE ART GALLERY
GALLERY DOLLS & DOLLS' HOSPITAL
Northumberland St North East La
TORRANCE: contemporary prints and watercolours
WEST & WILDE BOOKSHOP: Fringe venue
DUNDAS BOOK SHOP
— KWEILIN: bright and fresh Chinese food
— DANIEL SHACKLETON : portraits
and Scottish history
Northumberland St South East La
ALAN DAY: especially 19th century furniture
KEEPERS: Franco-Scottish game and fish
ANDREW PRINGLE: bookseller
ROYAL SCOTS CLUB: Fringe venue

CHAIRS
PO
Dundas Street
LAMONT
E GALLERY:
temporary art
West Lane
CONSERVATION CENTRE
URNE FINE ART:
th century paintings
FLAMINGO: dress hire

Northumberland Street

Nelson Street
Dublin
Meuse
BUNTOMS: Thai
hot and good
Northumberland
Place Lane
LINDEN
INSCAPE: dried flowers
and baskets

Nelson Street

Dublin

Broughton
Market

UMBERTO'S: good pasta

UMBERTO'S DELI:
sandwiches/snacks

Street

Dublin
Street
La S

ST PAUL &

Place

Abercromby

New Town

NATIONAL PORTRAIT
GALLERY
Scottish royalty, artists
and philosophers

CUNNINGH
hatter found
North

4

Row

Gardens

Queen Street Gardens East

E

Queen Street

BBC

N Saint

ROYAL COLLEGE OF
PHYSICIANS: Fringe venue

Thistle Street Lane
North East

Thistle Street

N Saint
& N Andrew St

Bus
Statio

TAXI

33

Hanover
Street

St Andrew Square

St David St

ST ANDREW &
ST GEORGE
Compact oval design

tique furniture

stle Street Lane North West

Thistle Street

histle Street Lane
South West

D

GEORGE HOTEL

George Street

No.5: 200 years ago the home of Wm.
Creech the pre-eminent publisher
and bookseller in Scotland.

St Andrew Square

TAXI

No.11 was home of
Hugo Arnot, who summoned
servants using gunshot after
a neighbour complained about
constantly hearing his bell

S Sain

5

rge Street

Hanover

Street

At the end of the last century several
people reported seeing the ghost of
Jane Vernell. She had been a corsetiere
in the street. The eerie figure walked up
and down impervious to the wind and rain

Rose Street

Rose Street
North Lane
North Lane

South St David Street

Rose Street South Lane

Meuse Lane

TAXI

L

Rose Street

North Lane

Restricted access

Rose Street South Lane

K

TAXI

Princes Street

200 ft high -
completed
in 1846

Waverley Bri

6

J

FLORAL CLOCK:
horological

ROYAL
SCOTTISH
ACADEMY

East Princes

**Street
Gardens**

SCOTT
MONUMENT

Cafés/Snacks | Pubs | Restaurants | Hotels | Cinemas | Theatres

The streets outlined in red
here are shown in greater
detail on page 15.

LRT CENTRAL BUSES

D See page 33   J See page 33
E 2/12 4/4A 10/10A 16/16A 17 18/18A 19/39 20
    22/25/73 23 27 30 42/46 45/47 81/81A/81B 82 82A 83
F 4/4A 5/51A 7 8 10/10A 11 14 15 16/16A 17 18A 19/39
    22/25/73 34/35 42/46 45/47 65 X66 74 87
K 2/12 3 4/4A 10/10A 11 15 16/16A 17 21 18/18A 23

EASTERN SCOTTISH

E EX1 X08 X10 X13 X12 16 17 18 X21 X23 X24 X26 27
    X28 X29 X32 37 37B 43 45 49 61 64 64A 65 65B 66 70
    72 74 76 77 X77 X79 80 80A 85 86 87 100 101 102
    104 106 108 112 113 124 125 129 145 273 274 276 281
F C5/C50 X08 X10 44/66 45 104 106 108 112 113 X12
D See page 33   J See page 33   [X13 124 X29 129 135

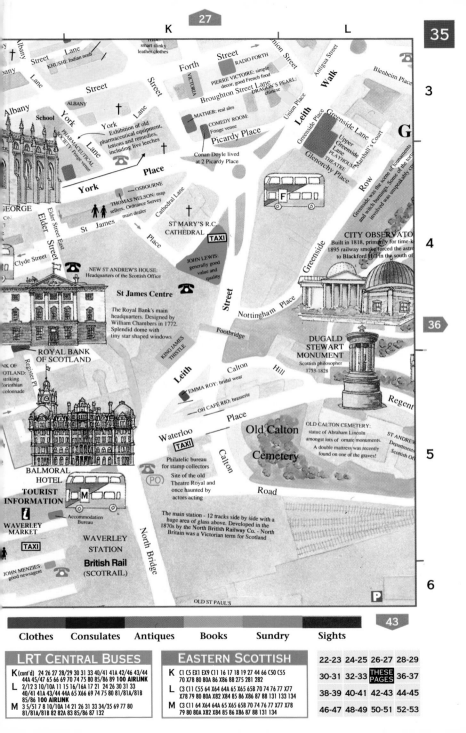

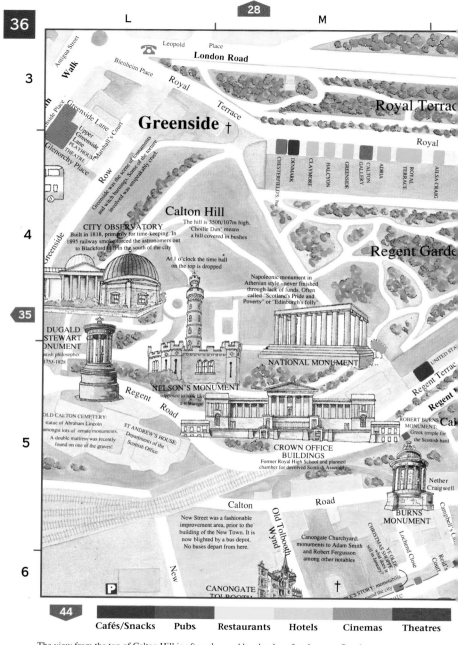

L   **M**

Antigua Street

Walk

☎ Leopold Place

London Road

Blenheim Place

Royal

Terrace

3

Royal Terrace

Greenside Lane

Greenside Place

Upper
Greenside
Lane
PLAYHOUSE
THEATRE

Marshall's Court

Glenorchy Place

ROW

Royal

CHESTERFIELD'S bar
DENMARK
CLAYMORE
HALCYON
GREENSIDE
CALTON GALLERY
ADRIA
ROYAL TERRACE
AILSA CRAIG

Greenside was the scene of tournaments and witch burnings. Some of the torture involved was unspeakably cruel.

Greenside †

Calton Hill

The hill is 350ft/107m high.
'Choille Dun' means
a hill covered in bushes

CITY OBSERVATORY
Built in 1818, primarily for time-keeping. In
1895 railway smoke forced the astronomers out
to Blackford Hill in the south of the city

4

Greenside

At 1 o'clock the time ball
on the top is dropped

Regent Garden

Napoleonic monument in
Athenian style - never finished
through lack of funds. Often
called "Scotland's Pride and
Poverty" or "Edinburgh's folly"

**DUGALD
STEWART
MONUMENT**
Scottish philosopher
1753-1828

NATIONAL MONUMENT

UNITED STA

Regent Terrac

NELSON'S MONUMENT
supposed to look like
a telescope

Regent

Road

Regent

OLD CALTON CEMETERY:
statue of Abraham Lincoln
amongst lots of ornate monuments.
A double mattress was recently
found on one of the graves!

ST ANDREW'S HOUSE:
Departments of the
Scottish Office

5

**ROBERT BURNS
MONUMENT:**
Greek temple for
the Scottish bard

**CROWN OFFICE
BUILDINGS**
Former Royal High School and planned
chamber for devolved Scottish Assembly

Nether
Craigwell

Campbell's Clo

Calton

Road

Old Tolbooth Wynd

**BURNS
MONUMENT**

Lochend Close

New Street was a fashionable
improvement area, prior to the
building of the New Town. It is
now blighted by a bus depot.
No buses depart from here.

YE OLDE
CHRISTMAS SHOPPE
sell it all year!

Canongate Churchyard:
monuments to Adam Smith
and Robert Fergusson
among other notables

Reid's

Court

6

New

🅿

CANONGATE
TOLBOOTH

†

E'S STORY: memorabilia
round the city

gate

Cafés/Snacks   **Pubs**   **Restaurants**   **Hotels**   **Cinemas**   **Theatres**

The view from the top of Calton Hill is often obscured by clouds or fog, but on a fine day
you get an excellent view of the city, Arthur's Seat and the Firth of Forth.
The road up the hill starts at the west end of the Crown Office Buildings, (under Nelson's Monument above).

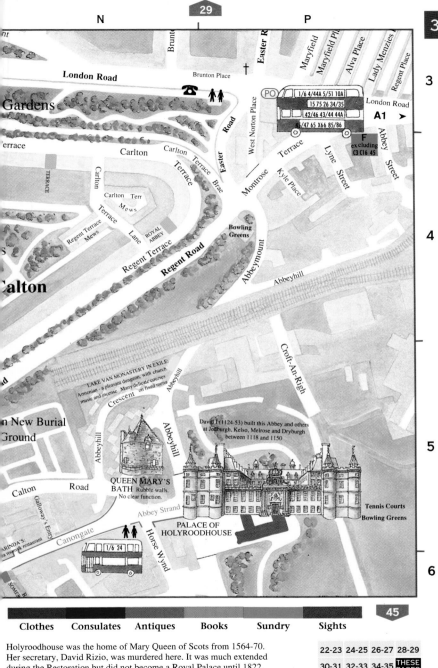

London Road

Brunton

Brunton Place

Easter R

Maryfield

Maryfield Place

Alva Place

Lady Menzies

Regent Place

London Road

A1

ex cluding
C3 C16 45

F

PO

1/6 4/44A 5/51 10A
15 75 26 34/35
42/46 43/44 44A
45/47 65 X66 85/86

Gardens

errace

Carlton

Carlton Terrace

Easter Road

West Norton Place

Montrose Terrace

Kyle Place

Lyne Street

Abbey Street

Carlton Terrace Brae

TERRACE

Carlton Terrace

Carlton Terr Mews

Regent Terrace Mews

Regent Terrace Lane

ROYAL ABBEY

Regent Terrace

Regent Road

Bowling Greens

Abbeymount

Abbeyhill

Abbeyhill

Calton

Croft-An-Righ

LAKE VAN MONASTERY IN EXILE
Armenian - a pleasant dungeon, with church
music and incense...Many delicate courses
on fixed menu.

Crescent

Abbeyhill

New Burial Ground

Abbeyhill

Abbeyhill

David I (1124-53) built this Abbey and others
at Jedburgh, Kelso, Melrose and Dryburgh
between 1118 and 1150

QUEEN MARY'S BATH Rubble walls.
No clear function.

Abbey Strand

PALACE OF HOLYROODHOUSE

Tennis Courts
Bowling Greens

Calton Road

Galloway's Entry

ARINDA'S:
a room and restaurant

Canongate

Horse Wynd

1/6 24

SOMER R

Clothes	Consulates	Antiques	Books	Sundry	Sights

Holyroodhouse was the home of Mary Queen of Scots from 1564-70.
Her secretary, David Rizio, was murdered here. It was much extended
during the Restoration but did not become a Royal Palace until 1822.
A number of impressive staterooms, bed chambers
and a picture gallery are open to the public.

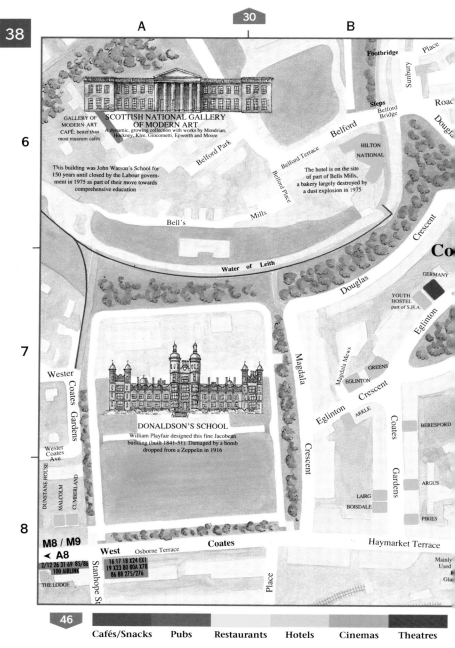

This is good place to start the Water of Leith Walk. From Belford Bridge the river winds through Dean village, passes under Dean Bridge (designed by Thomas Telford around 1830 and built from Craigleith stone) and continues on down a leafy valley to Stockbridge. Though small, the river was an important source of power, and at one time there were eleven watermills on this stretch of the river.

Murrayfield (page 57) is a short way off the map on the A8.
Edinburgh Airport is 8 miles out from here (see page 66).

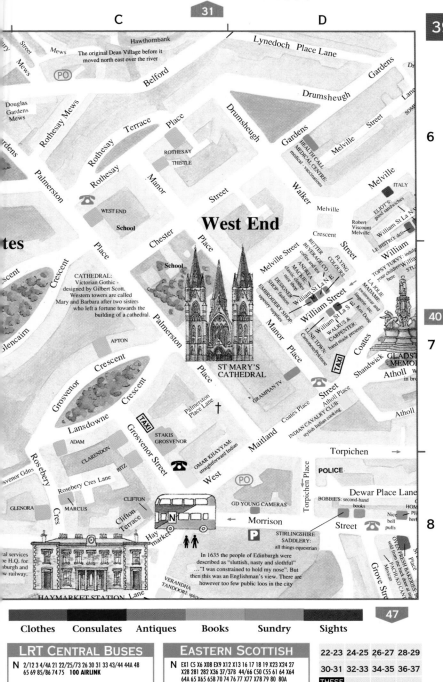

C

D

6

Lynedoch Place Lane

Hawthornbank

The original Dean Village before it
moved north east over the river

(PO)

Mews

Belford

Place

Drumsheugh

Gardens

Douglas
Gardens
Mews

Rothesay Mews

Terrace

Place

Drumsheugh

Gardens

Melville

Street

Palmerston

Rothesay

ROTHESAY

THISTLE

Manor

Rothesay

Street

Walker

Melville

HEALTH CALL
MEDICAL CENTRE:
medical • vaccinations

ITALY

Melville

ELIOT'S:
good sandwiches

Robert
Viscount
Melville

William St La N

WEST END

School

Chester

Place

West End

Crescent

Street

LE BISTRO: deli

William

tes

Place

School

Melville Street

BETTER
BEVERAGE CO:
coffee and tea

FLYING
COLOURS

TOPSY TURVY: indulge
your children

MAMME:
swimwear and
lingerie, inc
Kari Dunn

LA JOLIE

here

STL

CATHEDRAL:
Victorian Gothic -
designed by Gilbert Scott.
Western towers are called
Mary and Barbara after two sisters
who left a fortune towards the
building of a cathedral.

Palmerston

ANDREA
MACHE:
classic shoes

DESIGNER
fashion

EMBROIDERY
SHOP: fashion
tapestry supplies

William St LANE

William Street

William St La S

LINE TOWN:
Conran residence

WALRUS &
CARPENTER:
hand made presents

Coates

40

7

AFTON

Crescent

Glencairn

Crescent

Place

Manor

Place

TAXI

Shandwick

GLADST
MEMOR

Atholl

in bro

ST MARY'S
CATHEDRAL

GRAMPIAN TV

Street

Coates

Atholl Place

Atholl

Grosvenor

Crescent

Crescent

Palmerston
Place Lane

Coates Place

INDIAN CAVALRY CLUB:
stylish Indian cooking

Lansdowne

Maitland

Torpichen

ADAM

CLARENDON

Grosvenor Street

STAKIS
GROSVENOR

RITZ

OMAR KHAYYAM:
straightforward Indian

West

POLICE

Torpichen Place

Rosebery

Cres

GLENORA

Rosebery Cres Lane

MARCUS

CLIFTON

CLIFTON
Terrace

(PO)

GD YOUNG CAMERAS

Morrison

Dewar Place Lane

BOBBIES: second-hand
books

Nice
bell
pulls

HOM
PH
her

8

al services
e H.Q. for
burgh and
w railway.

N

Hay

Haymarket

P

Street

STIRLINGSHIRE
SADDLERY:
all things equestrian

In 1635 the people of Edinburgh were
described as "sluttish, nasty and slothful"
..."I was constrained to hold my nose". But
then this was an Englishman's view. There are
however too few public loos in the city

Grove Stre

OVEN
FRESH BAKERIES:
sold from the back door at the

FRECHI KOL CAND

Mexican

HAYMARKET STATION

Lane

VERANDHA
TANDOORI: spicy

Place

47

| Clothes | Consulates | Antiques | Books | Sundry | Sights |

LRT CENTRAL BUSES

N 2/12 3 4/4A 21 22/25/73 26 30 31 33 43/44 44A 48
65 69 85/86 74 75 **100 AIRLINK**

EASTERN SCOTTISH

N EX1 C5 X6 X08 EX9 X12 X13 16 17 18 19 X23 X24 27
X28 281 282 X36 37/37B 44/66 C50 C55 61 64 X64
64A 65 X65 65B 70 74 76 77 X77 X78 79 80 80A
X82 X84 85 86 X86 87 88 273 274 276

22-23	24-25	26-27	28-29
30-31	32-33	34-35	36-37
THESE PAGES	40-41	42-43	44-45
46-47	48-49	50-51	52-53

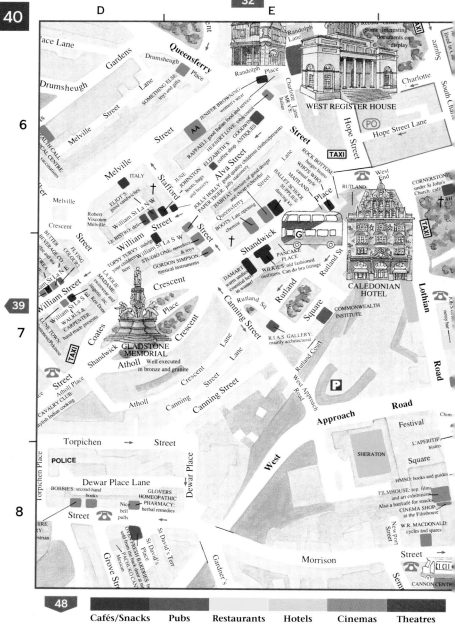

39
48

| Cafés/Snacks | Pubs | Restaurants | Hotels | Cinemas | Theatres |

The area above William Street (D7 above) is a good hunting ground for shops and cafés.
Lack of space has prevented some excellent shops being included.

If you join the West Approach Road here (E7 above) it
whisks you over a mile down to Dalry before you can leave it.

King's Stables Road (G7 above) was the site of a Royal Mews during the
jousting tournaments held here in the reign of James IV.

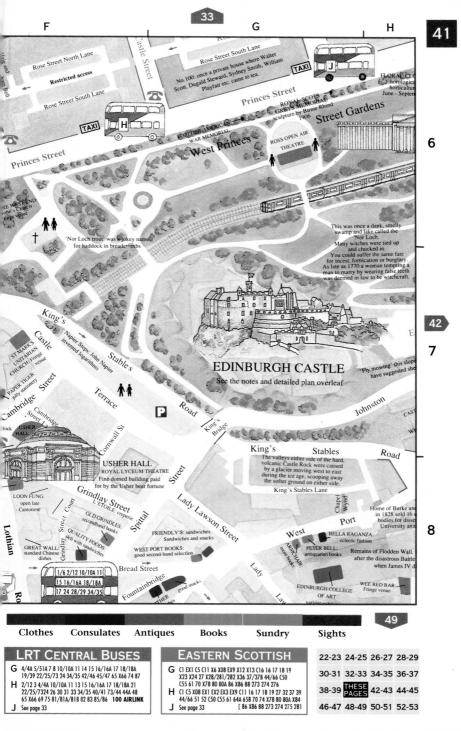

F   G   H

Rose Street North Lane

Restricted access

Rose Street South Lane

Castle Street

Rose Street South Lane

No. 100: once a private house where Walter
Scott, Dugald Steward, Sydney Smith, William
Playfair etc. came to tea.

TAXI J

TAXI H

Princes Street

FLORAL CLOCK
horological
horticulture
June - September

SCOTTISH AMERICAN
WAR MEMORIAL

ROYAL SCOTS
GREYS MEMORIAL
sculpture by Birnie Rhind
1906

Street Gardens

Princes Street

West Princes

ROSS OPEN AIR
THEATRE

6

† RE WEST END
John's Church
ringe venue

'Nor Loch trout' was a jokey name
for haddock in breadcrumbs

This was once a dank, smelly
swamp and lake called the
'Nor Loch.
Many witches were tied up
and chucked in.
You could suffer the same fate
for incest, fornication or burglary.
As late as 1770 a woman tempting a
man to marry by wearing false teeth
was deemed in law to be witchcraft.

King's

Castle

Napier Steps: John Napier
invented logarithms

Stables

ST MARK'S
UNITARIAN
CHURCH: Fringe
venue

PAPER TIGER:
jolly stationery

Terrace

Cambridge Street

Cambridge
Street studio

USHER
HALL

lock

EDINBURGH CASTLE
See the notes and detailed plan overleaf

Fly mowing this slope
have suggested she

42

7

Cornwall St

King's
Bridge

Road

Johnston

King's   Stables

Road

The valleys either side of the hard,
volcanic Castle Rock were caused
by a glacier moving west to east
during the ice age, scooping away
the softer ground on either side.
King's Stables Lane

USHER HALL
ROYAL LYCEUM THEATRE
Fine domed building paid
for by the Usher beer fortune

Grindlay Street

L'ETOILE: creperie

LOON FUNG:
open late
- Cantonese

Spittal Street

Street

Lady Lawson Street

Chapel Wynd

Home of Burke and
in 1828 sold 16
bodies for disse
University ana

Grindlay Street Court

OLD GRINDLES:
secondhand books

QUALITY FOODS:
deli with sandwiches

FRIENDLY'S: sandwiches
Sandwiches and snacks

WEST PORT BOOKS:
good second-hand selection

West   Port

ARMCHAIR:
more books

BELLA RAGAZA:
eclectic fashion

PETER BELL:
antiquarian books

Remains of Flodden Wall,
after the disastrous Battle
when James IV a

8

GREAT WALL:
standard Chinese
dishes

Lothian Ro

1/6 2/12 10/10A 11

15 16/16A 18/18A

17 24 28/29 34/35

Bread Street

Fountainbridge

Lady

Lady Law

good snacks

EDINBURGH COLLEGE
OF ART
various

WEE RED BAR:
Fringe venue

Clothes   Consulates   Antiques   Books   Sundry   Sights

49

LRT CENTRAL BUSES

G 4/4A 5/51A 7 8 10/10A 11 14 15 16/16A 17 18/18A
19/39 22/25/73 24 34/35 42/46 45/47 65 X66 74 87

H 2/12 3 4/4A 10/10A 11 13 15 16/16A 17 18/18A 21
22/25/7324 26 30 31 33 34/35 40/41 73/44 44A 48
65 X66 69 75 81/81A/81B 82 83 85/86 100 AIRLINK

See page 33

EASTERN SCOTTISH

G C1 EX1 C5 C11 X6 X08 EX9 X12 X13 C16 16 17 18 19
X23 X24 27 X28/281/282 X36 37/37B 44/66 C50
C55 61 70 X78 80 80A 86 X86 88 273 274 276

H C1 C5 X08 EX1 EX2 EX3 EX9 C11 16 17 18 19 27 32 37 39
44/66 51 52 C50 C55 61 64A 65B 70 74 X78 80 80A X84

J See page 33   [86 X86 88 273 274 275 281]

22-23	24-25	26-27	28-29
30-31	32-33	34-35	36-37
38-39	THESE PAGES	42-43	44-45
46-47	48-49	50-51	52-53

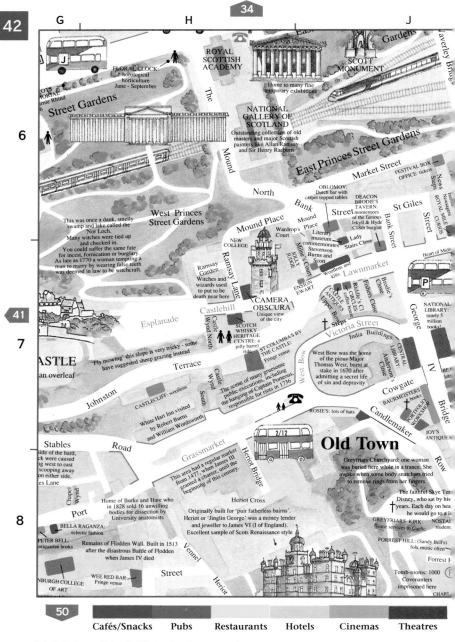

G **H** **J**

ROYAL SCOTTISH ACADEMY
Home to many fine temporary exhibitions

SCOTT MONUMENT

FLORAL CLOCK: horological horticulture June - September

Street Gardens

NATIONAL GALLERY OF SCOTLAND
Outstanding collection of old masters and major Scottish painters like Allan Ramsay and Sir Henry Raeburn

East Princes Street Gardens

6

Market Street

FESTIVAL BOX OFFICE: tickets

News Steps

North

West Princes Street Gardens

Bank

Mound Place

Street

St Giles

OBLOMOV: Dutch bar with carpet topped tables

DEACON BRODIE'S TAVERN: mementoes of the famous Jekyll & Hyde' C18th burglar

ROYAL MILE CURIOS

This was once a dank, smelly swamp and lake called the 'Nor Loch. Many witches were tied up and chucked in. You could suffer the same fate for incest, fornication or burglary. As late as 1770 a woman tempting a man to marry by wearing false teeth was deemed in law to be witchcraft.

Wardrop's Court

Literary museum commemorates Stevenson Burns and Scott

Lady Stairs Close

Bank Street

NEW COLLEGE

JOLLY JUDGE

Milne's Court

Woollens and kilts

Heart of Midl

Ramsay Lane

Ramsay Garden
Witches and wizards used to put to be death near here

Mound Place

ENSIGN EWART

Lawnmarket

Brodie's Close

Riddle's Cl

Fisher's Close

George

NATIONAL LIBRARY: nearly 5 million books!

CAMERA OBSCURA
Unique view of the city

Castlehill

CASTLE Wynd North

SCOTCH WHISKY HERITAGE CENTRE: a jolly barrel ride

ST COLUMBA'S BY THE CASTLE: Fringe venue

CASTLE BARNS coffee house

IV

41

Esplanade

Steps

India Buildings

Victoria Street

CENTRAL LIBRARY/ Anderson's Close

BE

7

CASTLE

an overleaf

'Fly mowing' this slope is very tricky - some have suggested sheep grazing instead

Terrace

Castle Wynd

South

The scene of many gruesome public executions, including the hanging of Captain Porteous, responsible for riots in 1736

West Bow

West Bow was the home of the pious Major Thomas Weir, burnt at stake in 1670 after admitting a secret life of sin and depravity

Cowgate

BAURMEISTERS books

Bridge

Johnston

CASTLECLIFF: woollens

White Hart Inn visited by Robert Burns and William Wordsworth

ROSIE'S: lots of hats

PORTFOLIO WORKSHOP

JOY'S ANTIQUES

Stables

side of the hard, ck were caused ng west to east scooping away on either side. es Lane

Road

Grassmarket

This area had a regular market from 1477, when James III granted a charter, until the beginning of this century.

Heriot Bridge

Candlemaker Row

Old Town

Greyfriars Churchyard: one woman was buried here while in a trance. She awoke when some body snatchers tried to remove rings from her fingers

Chapel Wynd

Port

Home of Burke and Hare who in 1828 sold 16 unwilling bodies for dissection by University anatomists

Heriot Cross

Originally built for 'puir fatherless bairns'. Heriot or 'Jinglin George' was a money lender and jeweller to James VI (I of England). Excellent sample of Scots Renaissance style

The faithful Skye Ter Disney, who sat by his years. Each day on hea he would go to a l

GREYFRIARS KIRK Some services in Gaelic

NOSTAl student

BELLA RAGANZA: eclectic fashion

PETER BELL: ntiquarian books

Remains of Flodden Wall. Built in 1513 after the disastrous Battle of Flodden when James IV died

FORREST HILL: (Sandy Bell's) folk music often ~

Forrest H

NBURGH COLLEGE OF ART

WEE RED BAR: Fringe venue

Street

Heriot

Vennel

Tomb-rooms: 1000 Covenanters imprisoned here

CHARL

8

Cafés/Snacks Pubs Restaurants Hotels Cinemas Theatres

This is the heart of historic Edinburgh and represents the greater part of the city up until the developments of the eighteenth century.

Deacon William Brodie was sentenced to death after several years of thieving from businesses and later the Excise. He was hanged on the very gibbet that he had re-designed - changed from a double ladder to a trap-door drop.

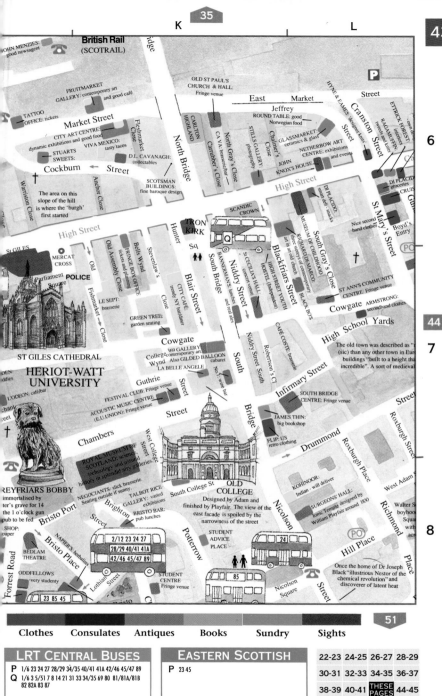

Clothes	Consulates	Antiques	Books	Sundry	Sights

LRT CENTRAL BUSES

P 1/6 23 24 27 28/29 34/35 40/41 41A 42/46 45/47 89
Q 1/6 3 5/51 7 8 14 21 31 33 34/35 69 80 81/81A/81B
   82 82A 83 87

EASTERN SCOTTISH

P 23 45

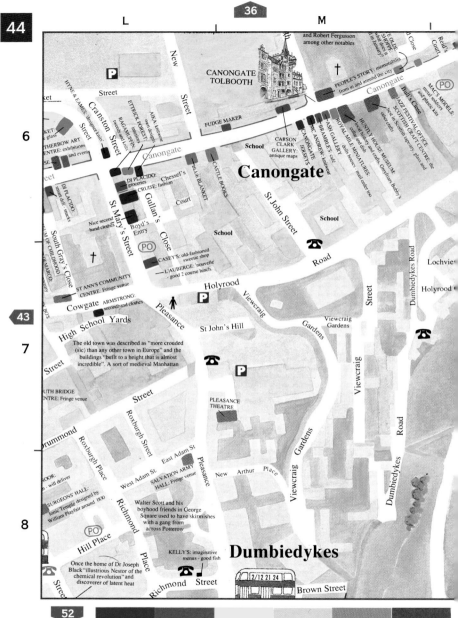

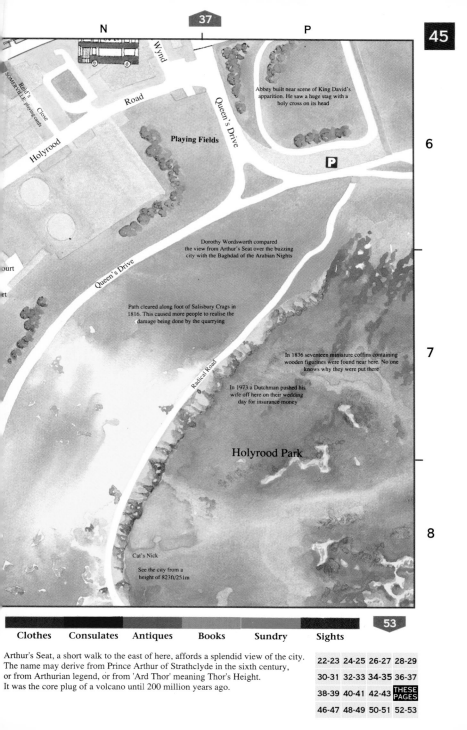

Abbey built near scene of King David's apparition. He saw a huge stag with a holy cross on its head

Reid's Close

SOMERVILLE playing fields

Holyrood Road

Wynd

Queen's Drive

Playing Fields

P

6

Dorothy Wordsworth compared the view from Arthur's Seat over the buzzing city with the Baghdad of the Arabian Nights

Queen's Drive

Path cleared along foot of Salisbury Crags in 1816. This caused more people to realise the damage being done by the quarrying

Radical Road

In 1836 seventeen miniature coffins containing wooden figurines were found near here. No one knows why they were put there

7

In 1973 a Dutchman pushed his wife off here on their wedding day for insurance money

Holyrood Park

8

Cat's Nick

See the city from a height of 823ft/251m

Clothes   Consulates   Antiques   Books   Sundry   Sights

Arthur's Seat, a short walk to the east of here, affords a splendid view of the city. The name may derive from Prince Arthur of Strathclyde in the sixth century, or from Arthurian legend, or from 'Ard Thor' meaning Thor's Height. It was the core plug of a volcano until 200 million years ago.

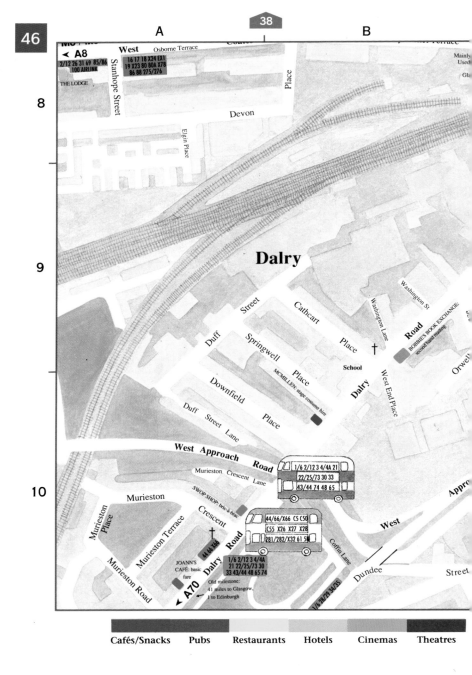

Dalry

Cafés/Snacks   Pubs   Restaurants   Hotels   Cinemas   Theatres

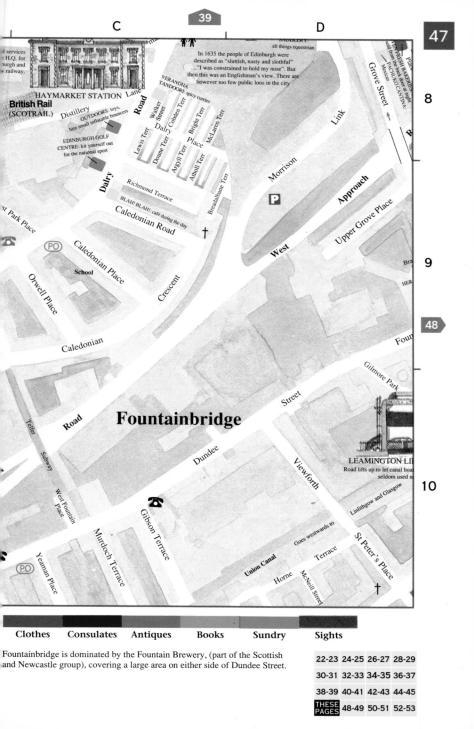

Clothes   Consulates   Antiques   Books   Sundry   Sights

Fountainbridge is dominated by the Fountain Brewery, (part of the Scottish and Newcastle group), covering a large area on either side of Dundee Street.

D   E

8

47

9

10

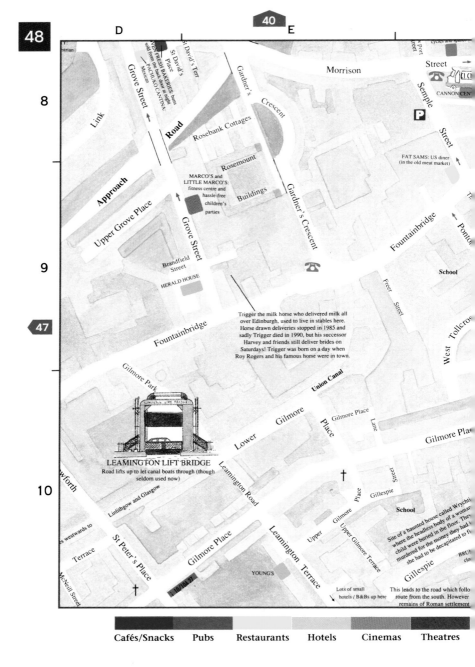

St David's Place
St David's Terr
WED FRESH BAKERIES buns sold from the back door at night
PACHIKO CANTINA: Mexican

Morrison   Street

Grove Street

Link

Gardner's

Crescent

Rosebank Cottages

Road

Rosemount

Approach

MARCO'S and LITTLE MARCO'S: fitness centre and hassle-free children's parties

Buildings

Upper Grove Place

Grove Street

Gardner's Crescent

Brandfield Street

HERALD HOUSE

Semple   Street

P

CANNON CEN

FAT SAMS: US diner (in the old meat market)

Fountainbridge

Ponto

School

Freer Street

West Tollcros

Trigger the milk horse who delivered milk all over Edinburgh, used to live in stables here. Horse drawn deliveries stopped in 1985 and sadly Trigger died in 1990, but his successor Harvey and friends still deliver brides on Saturdays! Trigger was born on a day when Roy Rogers and his famous horse were in town.

Fountainbridge

Gilmore Park

Union Canal

Gilmore

Lower   Gilmore   Place

Gilmore Place   Lane

Gilmore Pla

LEAMINGTON LIFT BRIDGE
Road lifts up to let canal boats through (though seldom used now)

Leamington Road

Gilmore   Place

†

Gillespie   Street

wforth

Linlithgow and Glasgow

s westwards to

Terrace

St Peter's Place

McNeill Street

Gilmore Place

†

Leamington Terrace

YOUNG'S

Upper   Gilmore   Place

Upper Gilmore Terrace

School

Site of a haunted house called Wrychit where the headless body of a woman child were buried in the floor. The murdered for the money they had she had to be decapitated to fi

BRU

clo

Gillespie

Lots of small hotels / B&Bs up here

This leads to the road which follo route from the south. However remains of Roman settlement

Cafés/Snacks   Pubs   Restaurants   Hotels   Cinemas   Theatres

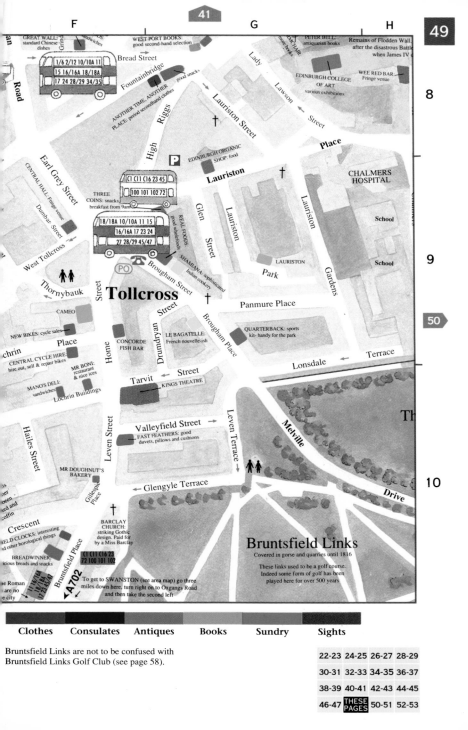

Bruntsfield Links are not to be confused with
Bruntsfield Links Golf Club (see page 58).

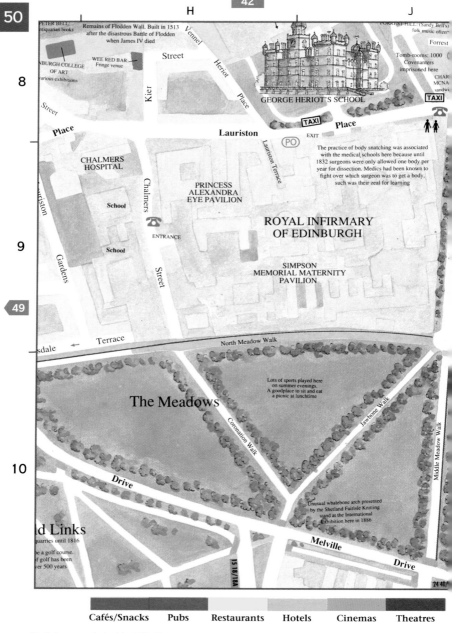

H

J

8

9

49

10

PETER BELL
antiquarian books

Remains of Flodden Wall. Built in 1513 after the disastrous Battle of Flodden when James IV died

FORREST HILL (Sandy Bell's) folk music often

EDINBURGH COLLEGE OF ART various exhibitions

WEE RED BAR Fringe venue

Forrest

Tomb-rooms: 1000 Covenanters imprisoned here

CHAR MCNA sandwi

Street

Vennel

Heriot

Place

TAXI

Street

Kier

GEORGE HERIOT'S SCHOOL

Place

TAXI

Lauriston

Place

EXIT

PO

Place

Lauriston Terrace

The practice of body snatching was associated with the medical schools here because until 1832 surgeons were only allowed one body per year for dissection. Medics had been known to fight over which surgeon was to get a body, such was their zeal for learning

CHALMERS HOSPITAL

Chalmers

PRINCESS ALEXANDRA EYE PAVILION

School

ROYAL INFIRMARY OF EDINBURGH

Lauriston

ENTRANCE

School

Street

SIMPSON MEMORIAL MATERNITY PAVILION

Gardens

sdale

Terrace

North Meadow Walk

The Meadows

Lots of sports played here on summer evenings. A goodplace to sit and eat a picnic at lunchtime

Coronation Walk

Jawbone Walk

Middle Meadow Walk

Drive

Unusual whalebone arch presented by the Shetland Fairisle Knitting stand at the International Exhibition here in 1886

ld Links

quarries until 1816

e a golf course. of golf has been er 500 years

Melville

Drive

15 18 /18A

24 40/

Cafés/Snacks	Pubs	Restaurants	Hotels	Cinemas	Theatres

Until they were drained in 1740, The Meadows were underwater and were called South Loch or Burgh Loch.

The cycle routes (purple lines) in this area afford an excellent route to the centre, avoiding much of the traffic.

Heriot's School was originally built for "puir fatherless bairns".
Heriot, or 'Jinglin Georgie', was a money lender and jeweller to James VI (James I of England).
The building is an excellent example of the Scots Renaissance style.

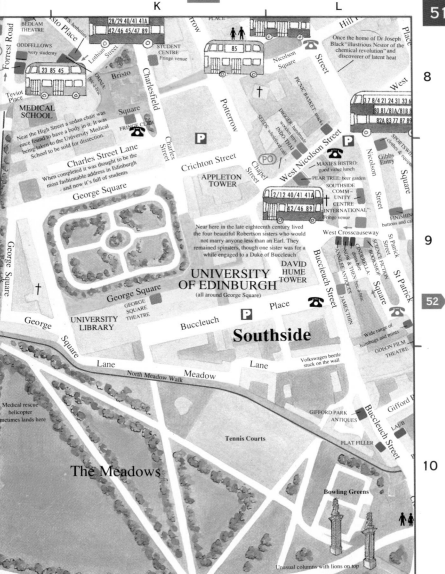

BEDLAM THEATRE

ODDFELLOWS very studenty

Forest Road

Bristo Place

St. herbalist

28/29 40/41 41A
42/46 45/47 89

STUDENT CENTRE Fringe venue

85

Nicolson Square

Once the home of Dr Joseph Black "illustrious Nestor of the chemical revolution" and discoverer of latent heat

West

8

Lothian Street

23 85 45

Bristo Square

Charlesfield

Charles Street

Teviot Place

MEDICAL SCHOOL

Near the High Street a sedan chair was once found to have a body in it. It was being taken to the University Medical School to be sold for dissection.

FRINGE CLUB

Potterrow

Charles Street Lane

When completed it was thought to be the most fashionable address in Edinburgh - and now it's full of students

George Square

P

Crichton Street

Chapel Street

PICNIC BASKET: snacks

ENGINE: landmark wooden toys

SPEED: wheelie craze

INFO THAI

PO

9 7 8/4 21 24 31 33 6
80 81/81A/81B
82A 83 77 87 89

SPORTSWEAR & equipment

Nicolson Street

Gibbs Entry

St Patrick Square

FINISHING buttons and ca

MAXIES BISTRO: good value lunch

PEAR TREE: beer garden

APPLETON TOWER

West Nicolson Street

SOUTHSIDE COMMUNITY CENTRE INTERNATIONAL: Fringe venue

9

Near here in the late eighteenth century lived the four beautiful Robertson sisters who would not marry anyone less than an Earl. They remained spinsters, though one sister was for a while engaged to a Duke of Buccleuch

UNIVERSITY OF EDINBURGH (all around George Square)

DAVID HUME TOWER

West Crosscauseway

Buccleuch Street

SCIENCE FICTION BOOKSHOP

CINDERELLA; SNOW & THEN: kidswear

ANNIE: ANTIQUES

JAMES THIN

St Patrick Street

52

George Square

George Square

George Square

UNIVERSITY LIBRARY

GEORGE SQUARE THEATRE

P

Place

Buccleuch

Southside

Wide range of humbugs and mints

ODEON FILM THEATRE

George Square

Lane

North Meadow Walk

Meadow

Lane

Volkswagen beetle stuck on the wall

Medical rescue helicopter sometimes lands here

GIFFORD PARK ANTIQUES

Buccleuch Street

Gifford

LAER

FLAT FILLER

10

Tennis Courts

The Meadows

Bowling Greens

Unusual columns with lions on top

41A

Clothes	Consulates	Antiques	Books	Sundry	Sights

The University has over 10,000 students and, together with the Royal Infirmary, exerts a considerable influence over this part of the city.

The Potterow (K8 above) was the home of a witch called Agnes Fynnie who was condemned in 1644 after a lifetime of sorcery. She seemed to be able to bring illness and misfortune to anyone who crossed her.

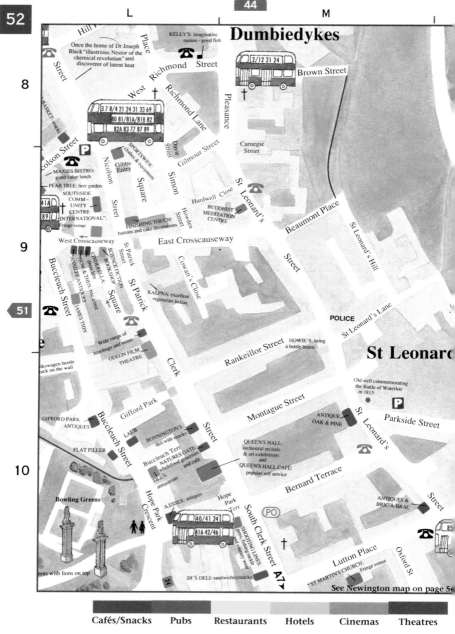

Dumbiedykes

St Leonard

The following labels appear on the map:

- Hill Place
- Street
- Once the home of Dr Joseph Black "illustrious Nestor of the chemical revolution" and discoverer of latent heat
- KELLY'S: imaginative menus - good fish
- West Richmond Street
- Richmond Lane
- Brown Street
- Pleasance
- Carnegie Street
- 2/12 21 24
- 3 7 8/4 21 24 31 33 69 / 80 81/81A/81B 82 / 82A 83 77 87 89
- Nicolson Street
- BASKET: snacks
- Nicolson Street
- MAXIES BISTRO: good value lunch
- PEAR TREE: beer garden
- SOUTHSIDE COMMUNITY CENTRE
- INTERNATIONAL": Fringe venue
- 41A
- 89
- Gibbs Entry
- SPORTSWISE: clothes & equipment
- Simon Square
- Davie Street
- Gilmour Street
- Hardwell Close
- BUDDHIST MEDITATION CENTRE
- St Leonard's Street
- Beaumont Place
- St Leonard's Hill
- FINISHING TOUCH: buttons and cake decorations
- Howden Street
- West Crosscauseway
- East Crosscauseway
- Buccleuch Street
- St Patrick Street
- SCIENCE FICTION BOOKSHOP
- CINDERELLA: dress hire
- NOW & THEN: bric-a-brac
- ANNIE'S ANTIQUES
- JAMES THIN
- St Patrick Square
- Cowan's Close
- KALPNA: excellent vegetarian Indian
- Volkswagen beetle stuck on the wall
- Wide range of humbugs and mints
- ODEON FILM THEATRE
- Clerk Street
- Rankeillor Street
- HOWIE'S: bring a bottle bistro
- POLICE
- St Leonard's Lane
- Old well commemorating the Battle of Waterloo in 1815
- GIFFORD PARK ANTIQUES
- Gifford Park
- Buccleuch Street
- LAUB
- BONNINGTON'S: deli with snacks
- FLAT FILLER
- Buccleuch Terr
- NATURES GATE: wholefood groceries and café
- TILL'S: antiquarian
- Montague Street
- QUEEN'S HALL: orchestral recitals & art exhibitions and QUEEN'S HALL CAFE: popular self service
- ANTIQUE OAK & PINE
- St Leonard's Street
- Parkside Street
- Bernard Terrace
- Bowling Greens
- Hope Park Crescent
- A.ESSEX: antiques
- Hope Park Terr
- 40/41 24 / 41A 42/46
- columns with lions on top
- DI'S DELI: sandwiches/snacks
- South Clerk Street
- PO
- ANTIQUES & BRIC-A-BRAC
- Street
- Lutton Place
- ST MARTIN'S CHURCH: Fringe venue
- Oxford St.
- A7
- SHOOTING LINES: films, cycling kit etc and country wear
- 85

See Newington map on page 56

Cafés/Snacks   Pubs   Restaurants   Hotels   Cinemas   Theatres

The area east of Buccleuch Street may seem a little run down but for many it has an appealing, bohemian, raffish quality.

The Newington map on page 56 adjoins the bottom of this page.

The A7 is the main route out of the city centre towards Dalkeith and Newcastle.

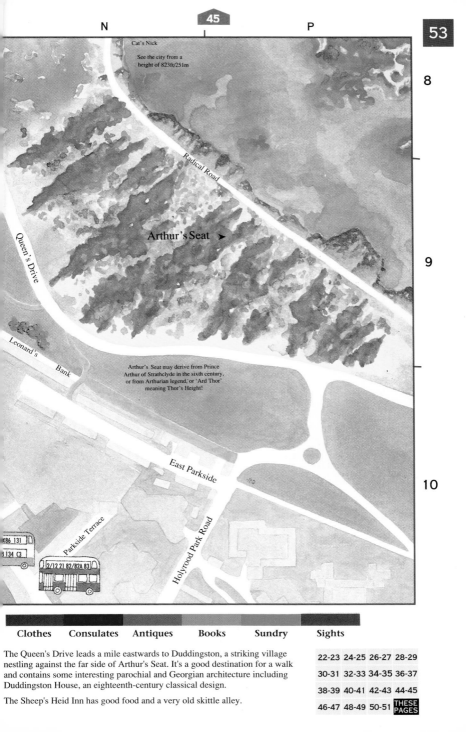

Cat's Nick

See the city from a
height of 823ft/251m

8

Radical Road

Queen's Drive

Arthur's Seat ➤

9

Leonard's Bank

Arthur's Seat may derive from Prince
Arthur of Strathclyde in the sixth century,
or from Arthurian legend, or 'Ard Thor'
meaning Thor's Height!

East Parkside

10

Parkside Terrace

Holyrood Park Road

X86 131

134 C3

2/12 21 82/82A 83

Clothes	Consulates	Antiques	Books	Sundry	Sights

The Queen's Drive leads a mile eastwards to Duddingston, a striking village
nestling against the far side of Arthur's Seat. It's a good destination for a walk
and contains some interesting parochial and Georgian architecture including
Duddingston House, an eighteenth-century classical design.

The Sheep's Heid Inn has good food and a very old skittle alley.

See key to colours and symbols on page 12.

This area is north east of the city centre and the bottom of this map adjoins pages 27-29.

LRT BUSES	
W	10/10A 16/16A 22/25/73
X	1/6 22/25/73
Y	1/6 7 17 22/25/73 87

EASTERN SCOTISH	
W	C16
X	C3
Y	C3 C16 C55
Z	C3 C16 C55

Although Leith finally lost its status as a separate burgh in 1920, it still feels entirely different in character to the city centre. It remained a working port, but decades of delapidation and often thoughtless demolition of old buildings left many streets and wharves bleak and forlorn. Young Leithers sought opportunities elsewhere, and many of the skills associated with the local maritime industry were lost or no longer required.

The last decade produced a variety of initatives to reverse this trend and a number of profess-ional and light industrial firms moved to Leith. Along with them came a number of bars and restaurants offering good food, usually in informal surroundings.

Today Leith is as independent in spirit as it ever was. Some see recent changes as little more than a façade, but in the main they are a source of pride and optimism. Leith is full of interest for the vistitor and should be explored on foot: merchants' houses, narrow alleys, warehouses and the smell of the sea are all testament to at least 700 years of maritime endeavour.

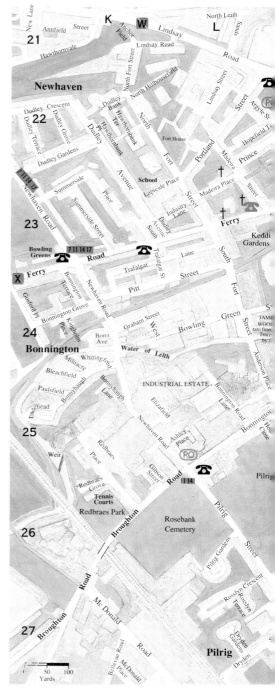

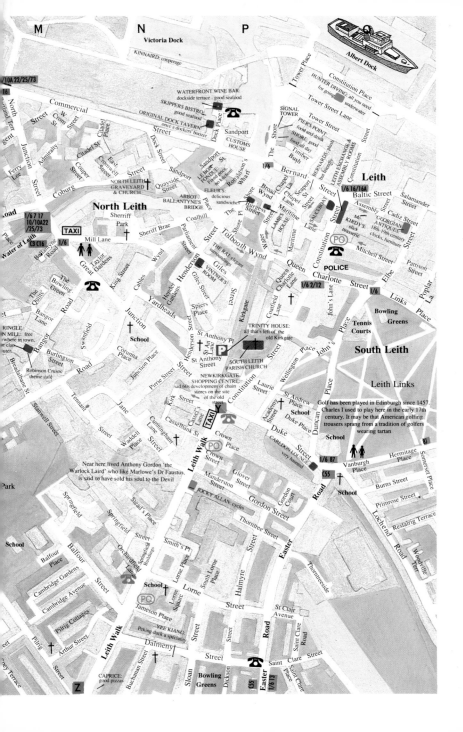

NEWINGTON

This area is south-east of the city centre and the top of this map adjoins pages 52-53.

It's full of commodius Victorian villas, many of which have been converted into hotels and guest houses. Causewayside has over a dozen antique shops - collectors of furniture and bric-à-brac should find a few bargains.

See key to colours and symbols on page 12.

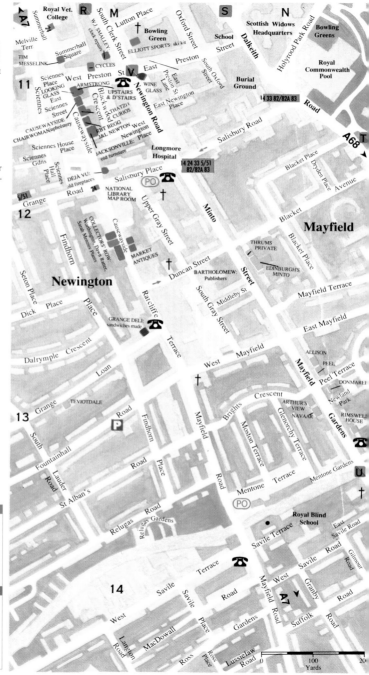

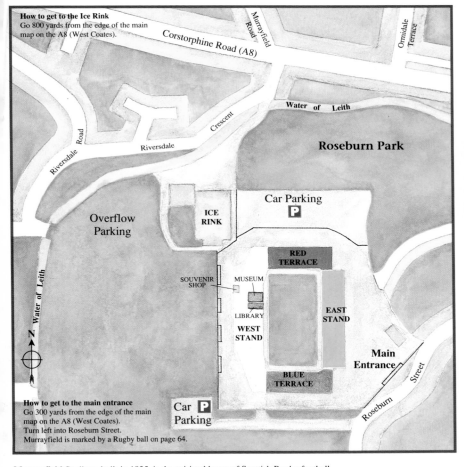

How to get to the Ice Rink
Go 800 yards from the edge of the main
map on the A8 (West Coates).

Murrayfield Road

Corstorphine Road (A8)

Ormidale Terrace

Water of Leith

Crescent

Riversdale Road

Riversdale

Roseburn Park

Car Parking
P

Overflow
Parking

ICE
RINK

N

Water of Leith

SOUVENIR
SHOP

MUSEUM

RED
TERRACE

LIBRARY

WEST
STAND

EAST
STAND

BLUE
TERRACE

**Main
Entrance**

Roseburn Street

How to get to the main entrance
Go 300 yards from the edge of the main
map on the A8 (West Coates).
Turn left into Roseburn Street.
Murrayfield is marked by a Rugby ball on page 64.

Car P
Parking

Murrayfield Stadium, built in 1925, is the spiritual home of Scottish Rugby football.
International rugby matches are played here throughout the season (which lasts from September - April).
Club matches are played each Saturday on the back pitches.
The **Murrayfield Museum** and **Reference Library** contain the history and development of Rugby.
Conducted tours available for 6 people or more by arrangement. Telephone to check opening times.
The **Souvenir Shop** sells leisure wear and memorabilia, so you can pretend you went to a match even if you didn't.
There are facilities for indoor and outdoor exhibitions, rallies, conferences and other events.

Nearby is **Murrayfield Ice Rink**, home of the **Murrayfield Racers** ice hockey club. Regular ice-skating sessions
available, also skate hire and tuition. Ice hockey matches most Sunday evenings. Telephone to check opening times
and admission charges.

Murrayfield Stadium
Roseburn Street
Edinburgh EH12
Tel: 031-337 9551
Telegrams: "Scrum Edinburgh"

Murrayfield Ice Rink
Riversdale Crescent
Edinburgh EH12
Tel: 031-337 6933

FIFE

NAME / DIRECTIONS	TELEPHONE	HOLES	YARDS		PUBLIC	MAP
Baberton						
Baberton Avenue, Juniper Green, 5 miles W on A70	031-453 4911	18	6140		No	**11**
Visitors require introduction by member						
Braidhills						
Braids Hill Approach, 4 miles S of city centre	031-447 3327	18	5731	No.1	Yes	**23**
Visitors welcome		18	4832	No.2		
Broomieknowe						
Bonnyrigg EH19, 6 miles SE of centre on A7						
Visitors welcome on weekdays	031-663 9317	18	6046		No	**33**
Bruntsfield Links						
Barnton Avenue, Davidsons Mains, 2 miles W on A90						
Visitors welcome on weekdays by appointment	031-336 1479	18	6407		No	**15**
Carrick Knowe						
Balgreen Road, Glendevon Park EH12						
Visitors welcome	031-337 1932	18	6299		Yes	**12**
Craigmillar Park						
Observatory Road EH9, 3 miles SE along A701						
Visitors welcome on weekdays, with conditions	031-667 0047	18	5846		No	**24**
Dalmahoy						
Near Kirknewton, 6 miles SW on A71	031-333 2055	18	5121	West	No	**7**
Visitors welcome		18	6664	East		
Deer Park						
Knightsbridge, near Livingston. 15 miles SW via M8						
Visitors welcome	0506-38843	18	6775		No	**3**
Duddingston						
3 miles SE of centre						
Visitors on weekdays only	031-661 7688	18	6647		No	**28**
Dunbar						
Half a mile E of Dunbar centre	0368 62317	18	6426		No	**44**
Visitors welcome						
Gifford						
A1 E to Haddington, then A6137 S for nearly 5 miles	062 081 267	9	6138		No	**38**
Visitors welcome except at certain times						

GOLF COURSES IN LOTHIAN

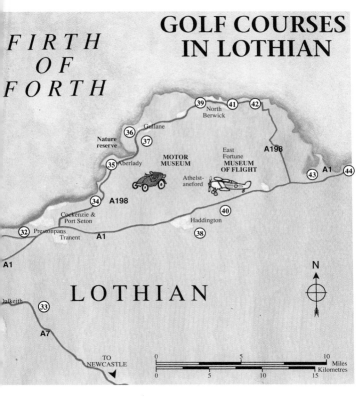

FIRTH OF FORTH

LOTHIAN

NAME / DIRECTIONS	TELEPHONE	HOLES	YARDS	PUBLIC	MAP
Glen					
21 miles NE on A198	0620 2221	18	6098	No	**42**
Visitors welcome					
Glencorse					
9 miles S on A701	0968 77189	18	5205	No	**22**
Visitors welcome					
Gullane	0620 842255	18	6466 No.1	No	**36**
18 miles NE via A1 and A198		18	6127 No.2		
Visitors welcome (Restrictions on No.1 course)		18	5128 No.3		
Haddington					
Half a mile E of Haddington via A1	0620 823627	18	6280	No	**40**
Visitors welcome (with booking)					
Harburn					
Off A70, 15 miles SW of city	0506 871256	18	5853	No	**5**
Visitors welcome	0506 871131				
Honourable Company of Edinburgh Golfers					
18 miles NE via A1 and A198	0620 842123	18	6941	No	**39**
Visitors welcome, with restrictions					
Kilspindie					
Aberlady, 15 miles NE via A1 and A198	0875 358/216	18	5410	Yes	**35**
Visitors welcome with booking					
Kingsknowe					
2 miles SW on A71	031-441 4030	18	5979	No	**16**
Visitors welcome on weekdays					
Liberton					
3 miles SE on A7	031-664 3309	18	5299	No	**29**
Visitors welcome except some weekday evenings					
Linlithgow					
South of Linlithgow, off M9	0506 842585	18	5858	Yes	**2**
Visitors welcome on most days					
Longniddry					
Longniddry, via A1 and A198	0875 52141	18	6210	No	**34**
Visitors welcome on most days	0875 52228				

GOLF COURSES IN LOTHIAN (continued)

NAME / DIRECTIONS	TELEPHONE	HOLES	YARDS	PUBLIC	MAP
Lothianburn					
5 miles S, off A702	031-445 2206	18	5720	No	21
Visitors welcome on weekdays					
Luffness New					
Aberlady, 17 miles NE via A1 and A198	0620 843336	18	6122	No	37
Visitors welcome by arrangement					
Merchants of Edinburgh					
Craiglockhart Hill EH10, 2 miles S off A702	031-447 1219	18	4889	No	19
Visitors require introduction by member					
Mortonhall					
2 miles S on A702	031-447 6974	18	6557	No	25
Visitors welcome with booking on weekdays					
Murrayfield					
2 miles W on A8	031-447 6974	18	5727	No	10
Visitors welcome on weekdays with introduction					
Musselburgh					
6 miles E via A1	031-665 2005	18	6623	No	31
Visitors welcome with booking					
Newbattle					
Abbey Road, Dalkeith, 7 miles SW on A7	031-663 2123	18	6012	No	30
Visitors welcome on weekdays except evenings					
North Berwick					
22 miles E via A1 and A198	0620 2135	18	6315	No	41
Visitors welcome					
Portobello					
3 miles E off A1	031-669 4361	9	2400	Yes	27
Visitors welcome except Saturdays in summer					
Prestonfield					
2 miles S, off Dalkeith Road	031-667 1273	18	6216	No	26
Visitors restricted at weekends	031-667 9665				
Pumpherston					
Near Uphall, 12 miles W via A8 and A89	0506 32869	9	5154	Yes	6
Visitors welcome with member					
Ratho Park					
Near Airport, 7 miles W on A71	031-333 1752	18	6028	No	8
Visitors welcome	1252				
Ravelston					
1 mile W, off A90 Queensferry Road	031-312 2486	9	5200	No	13
Visitors welcome					
Royal Burgess					
4 miles W, on Whitehouse Rd, N of Barnton roundabout	031-339 2075	18	6604	No	14
Visitors welcome on weekdays					
Royal Musselburgh					
Prestonpans, 7 miles E via A1 and A198	0875 810276	18	6237	No	32
Visitors welcome on weekdays					
Silverknowes					
2 miles NW, off Parkway EH4	031-336 5359	18	6210	No	18
Visitors welcome with booking					
Swanston					
Swanston Road, 3 miles S via A702	031- 445 2239	18	5024	No	20
Visitors restricted at weekends					
Torphin Hill					
Torphin Road, Colinton EH13, 5 miles SW on A70	031-441 1100	18	5030	No	17
Visitors restricted during competitions					
Turnhouse					
6 miles W via A8 and A9080, near airport	031-339 1014	18	6171	No	9
Visitors restricted - by arrangement					
Uphall					
14 miles W off M8	0506 856404	18	6250	No	4
Visitors welcome					
West Lothian					
Airngath Hill, Linlithgow	0506 826030	18	6578	No	1
Visitors welcome evenings/weekends by arrangement					
Winterfield					
West of Dunbar, off A1	0368 62280	18	5035	Yes	43
Visitors welcome					

WALKING TOURS

Ladies / Witchery Tours
031-225 6745
Must book.
Meet: outside Witchery restaurant, Castlehill.
Murder & Mystery *19.00, 22.00*
Graveyard Walks *23.00*

Calton Walking Tours
031-652 2269
Tours by appointment only.

Edinburgh Walking Tour Co.
031-220 2086
Specialist walks by full members of the Scottish Tourist
Guides Association (see below). Foreign language tours
by arrangement. Also science and theatre walks.
Meet: mornings - outside Information Centre above
Waverley Shopping Centre; afternoons - outside Scotch
Whisky Heritage Centre, Castlehill.
Old Town *11.00, 13.00*

Mercat Walking Tours
031-661 4541
Meet: by Mercat Cross beside St Giles Cathedral.
Royal Mile *11.00, 14.00*
Ghosthunter Trail *21.30*
Ghosts and Ghouls *19.00, 20.00*

New Town Conservation Centre
13a Dundas Street
031-557 5222
Interior of a New Town house*

Pub Walk *(summer)*
031-717 3037
Meet: at the foot of The Mound.
Sunday, Monday, Tuesday and Thursday 20.00

Robin's Walking Tours
031-661 0125
Meet: by water fountain above Waverley Shopping
Centre.
Ghosts and Ghouls *19.00*
New Town *14.00 (summer)*
Old Town and Royal Mile *10.00, 11.00 (all year)*
Port of Leith*
Royal Botanic Gardens*
Holyrood Royal Park*

Scottish Wildlife Trust
031-226 4602
Meet: outside Holyrood Lodge.
Holyrood Royal Park* *13.30 (Wednesdays only)*

Tailor-Made Tours
Day: (0592) 754411 ext.6153, Evenings: 031- 557 1362
Edinburgh Castle Archaeology*
(Evenings and weekends only)

* - Telephone for details

Booking
In most cases no booking is required. Some require
booking, because they are either very popular or by
prior arrangement only.
Larger groups should always book.

Times
Quoted times are for the summer but often change.
Especially out of season, telephone the guides or check
with the Tourist Information Centre above Waverley
Shopping Centre to save yourself a wasted journey.
The price of a 1-2 hour guided walk is usually
£3.00 - £5.00.

Guides
If you want to hire the services of a qualified guide for
yourself or your group you should contact the
Scottish Tour Guides Association
Edinburgh Agent:
Bob Motion, 78 Promenade,
Joppa, Edinburgh EH15 2EL
Telephone & fax: 031-669 6433.

Guides can be booked for anytime from half a day, to
several days for an extended tour. Naturally, particular
guides have specialist areas of knowledge and expertise.
In Edinburgh, guides are available with skills in the
following languages:

Czech	German	Portuguese
Danish	Italian	Russian
Dutch	Japanese	Spanish
French	Norwegian	Swedish

Many of the guides will undertake tours either in their
own cars or in vehicles provided by the customer.

BUS TOURS

LRT (LOTHIAN REGIONAL TRANSPORT)
031-220 4111 or 031-554 4494
Tickets from Tourist Offices, Waverley Ticket Office,
Waverley Bridge or LRT offices at 14 Queen Street
Classic Tour: in *summer* this city centre tour runs all
day *every 15 minutes from 9.10 to 17.10.*
There is a less frequent service in winter.
The tour goes round all the major sights and you can get
on and off where you like.
Historic Edinburgh: 2½ hours including guided tour of
either Holyroodhouse or the Castle depending on the
day.
Departs: *10.30 daily* from Waverley Bridge.
Sea, City and Hills: *(summer only)* tour of the villages
and outskirts of the city. Includes Newhaven,
Duddingston and Pentland foothills.
Departs *10.45, 13.30* and *15.30* from Waverley Bridge.

Guide Friday
031-556 2244
Very similar to LRT Classic Tour but a little more
expensive because there is a separate guide rather than a
driver/guide.

Scotline Tours
031-557 0162 - Bookings preferred.
City tour departs *09.00 (also 14.00 in summer)* from
Waverley Bridge and lasts 3-4 hours.
Ticket includes entrance to Holyroodhouse and Castle.
Passengers can be picked up from hotels or guest houses.

Eastern Scottish Coach Tours
031-558 1616/7
Wide range of tours covering the whole of Scotland.

FIFE

LEITH MAP

MAIN MAP

NEWING MAP

MURRAYFIELD (1 km out on A8)
Rugby Union, Ice Hockey and Curling

Battlefield
(date above)

C HOPETOUN HOUSE (East Wing)

E FORTH RAIL BRIDGE

A LINLITHGOW
Extensive, atmospheric remains of Gothic/Renaissance fortified palace. Canal Museum: nostalgic exhibits of better times on the Union Canal.

B HOUSE OF THE BINNS
Medieval building converted during 17th century into a fine country house.

C HOPETOUN HOUSE
Large and splendid Adam mansion with state rooms, garden and museums.

D DUNFERMLINE ABBEY & CARNEGIE MUSEUM
Impressive nave of medieval Benedictine abbey. Andrew Carnegie Museum (in his birthplace) shows the upbringing of the famous steel magnate and philanthropist.

E FORTH BRIDGES
Two modern wonders of the industrial world. The rail bridge was finished in 1890. The road bridge (1964) has a central span of 3300ft.

F RATHO
Centre for canal trips up and down the Union Canal. Food and drink available from the Bridge Inn.

G DALMENY HOUSE
Rothschild furniture collection in a large early 19th century Gothic Revival manor. Home of the Earl of Rosebery.

H ABERDOUR CASTLE
Remains of a 14th-16th century castle.

I CRAMOND
Picturesque village with famous inn. Various Roman remains.

J ZOO
Two thousand animals of all sizes in eighty acres of land on the side of Corstorphine Hill. Largest self-supporting penguin colony in the world. Lots of wild cats - leopards, lions, tigers. Open every day.

K SWANSTON
Tricky to find - perhaps deliberately. Group of small whitewashed cottages at foot of the Pentland Hills, one of which was R.L.Stevenson's holiday home for many years.

L HILLEND SKI CENTRE
Chairlift and longest artificial ski slope in Britain. Places to eat nearby include The Steading bar/restaurant.

M DUDDINGSTON
Picturesque village on east side of Arthur's Seat - a 2 mile walk from centre over the hill or along old railway track. See the Kirk, Loch and Session House. The latter enabled a watch to be mounted over the graveyard.

N BUTTERFLY FARM
Lots of pretty butterflies, some of which are very large. Also birds, spiders and insects.

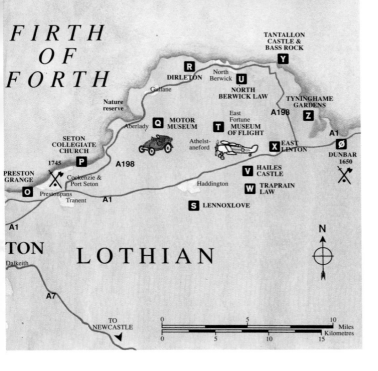

FIRTH
OF
FORTH

TANTALLON
CASTLE &
BASS ROCK
Y

R DIRLETON
North
Berwick
U

NORTH
BERWICK LAW

TYNINGHAME
GARDENS
Z

Nature
reserve

A198

Gullane

Aberlady

Q MOTOR
MUSEUM

East
Fortune

T MUSEUM
OF FLIGHT

A1
Ø

SETON
COLLEGIATE
CHURCH

Athelst-
aneford

X EAST
LINTON

DUNBAR
1650

1745 **P**

A198

Cockenzie &
Port Seton

V HAILES
CASTLE

PRESTON
GRANGE

O Prestonpans

Tranent A1

Haddington

W TRAPRAIN
LAW

A1

S LENNOXLOVE

TON

Dalkeith

LOTHIAN

N

A7

TO
NEWCASTLE

0   5   10 Miles
0   5   10   15 Kilometres

K SWANSTON

Y TANTALLON CASTLE

O PRESTON GRANGE
Mining museum: history of Lothian coal fields. Clever reconstructions of early 20th century mining life. Lots of noisy machinery.

P SETON COLLEGIATE CHURCH
Interesting 15th century church with a truncated octagonal tower and unusual choir.

Q MYRETON MOTOR MUSEUM
Vintage and veteran cars, vans and motor bikes.

R DIRLETON
Very pretty village with a ruined medieval castle and a number of significant later buildings.

S LENNOXLOVE
Turreted country house in large park. Part of it dates from 15th century, but mainly 17th/18th. Portraits by Raeburn, Van Dyck and Lely. Other items of interest include Rudolph Hess's map of Scotland and Mary, Queen of Scots' death mask.

T MUSEUM OF FLIGHT
Used to be a base for transatlantic airship crossings. Exhibits include a Spitfire, a Comet and a Vulcan bomber.

U NORTH BERWICK LAW
600ft high mound which dominates the local scenery. Various remains of old defences. Good views from the top - site of a Napoleonic warning beacon.

V HAILES CASTLE
Ruined castle, built and then enlarged between the 13th and 15th centuries.

W EAST LINTON
Idyllic Preston Mill, a restored, pantiled water mill and kiln. Also the Phantassie Doocot, a beehive-shaped dovecote.

X TRAPRAIN LAW
Large, isolated hill – the core of an old volcano. Settled since the Bronze Age and home during the Roman period of the Votadini tribe.

Y TANTALLON CASTLE & BASS ROCK
Impressive 14th-century fortress on cliff edge. Very bleak in winter. Large dovecote. Bass Rock rises 350ft from the sea. Large population of gannets, puffins and other sea-birds.

Z TYNINGHAME GARDENS
Excellent gardens and ruined Norman church of St Baldred, reached through an 18th-century avenue of lime trees.

Ø DUNBAR
Interesting old royal burgh, now mainly a holiday resort. Remnants of a ruined castle, Lauderdale House (designed by Robert Adam) and cobbled quays are all worth seeing.

ADVICE / CRISIS
Emergency - Fire, Police, Ambulance 999
Samaritans 031-225 3333
Womens Aid, 97 Morrison Street EH3 ..... 031-229 1419
Citizens' Advice Bureau, 58 Dundas Street EH3 ..... 031-557 1500

HOSPITALS / DENTAL
Royal Infirmary, 1 Lauriston Place EH3 ..... 031-229 2477
Western General, Crewe Road South EH4 (Off map) 031-332 2525
Leith Hospital, Mill Lane EH6 ..... 031-554 4433
Royal Hospital for Sick Children, 9 Sciennes Road EH9 ..... 031-667 1991
Dental Hospital, 31 Chambers Street EH1 ..... 031-225 9511

POLICE

LOTHIAN AND BORDERS POLICE
Police Headquartes, Fettes Avenue EH4 ..... 031-311 3131
Gayfield Square Police Station, 1 Gayfield Square EH1 ..... 031-556 9270
West End Police Station, Torphichen Place EH3 ..... 031-229 2323
Leith Police Station, Queen Charlotte Street EH6 ..... 031-554 9350
South Side Police Station, Causewayside EH9 ..... 031-667 3361

LOST PROPERTY
Police 031-311 3141
British Rail 031-556 2477
LRT Buses 031-554 4494
Eastern Scottish Buses 031-556 8126

DRY CLEANERS
Pullars, 23 Frederick Street EH2 ..... 031-225 8095
Munro, 46 Shandwick Place EH2 ..... 031-225 2088
(both companies have other branches)

LAUNDERETTES
Tarvit Launderette, 7/9 Tarvit Street EH3 ..... 031-229 6382
The Automatic, 38 Comely Bank Place EH4 ..... 031-332 6830
Bendix Self-Service, 13 South Clerk Street EH8 ..... 031-667 5844

INFORMATION (See also 'Travel & Tourism, Tickets' on page 76)
Tourist Centre, Waverley Market:
Tourist Information 031-557 2727
Accommodation Service 031-557 1700
Edinburgh Festival Fringe, 170 High Street EH1 ..... 031-226 5257
Edinburgh Festival Society, 21 Market Street EH1 ..... 031-226 4001
Edinburgh Military Tattoo, 22 Market Street EH1 ..... 031-225 1188
Edinburgh International Jazz Festival, 116 Canongate EH8 ..... 031-557 1642

RELIGIOUS SERVICES: INFORMATION
Church of Scotland (Offices), 121 George Street EH2 ..... 031-225 5722
Scottish Episcopal Church, Diocesan Centre, Walpole Hall, Chester Street EH3 ..... 031-226 3358
St. Mary's Catholic Cathedral Church, 61 York Place EH1 ..... 031-556 0027
The Central Mosque, 50 Potterow EH8 ..... 031-667 0140
Synagogue Chambers, 4 Salisbury Road EH16 ..... 031-667 3144

OPENING HOURS
Shops: Generally *Monday – Saturday 9.00 – 17.30*
(Late opening on *Thursday until 19.00 or 20.00*)
Banks: Bank of Scotland / Royal Bank of Scotland
Monday – Wednesday, Friday 9.15 – 16.45, Thursday 9.15 – 17.30
Clydesdale Bank:
Monday – Wednesday, Friday 9.15 – 16.00, Thursday 9.15 – 17.30
Other banks have similar hours.
Licensed Premises (Pubs, bars and off-licences):
Many are open all day, but generally:
Monday – Saturday 11.00 – 14.30, then 17.00 – 23.00 or midnight
Sunday 12.30 – 14.30 , then 18.30 – 23.00

TRANSPORT
Edinburgh Airport (see page 66 for more information) 031-333 1000
British Rail- Waverley Station 031-556 2451
Bus Information
Lothian Regional Transport 'LRT' 031-220 4111
(Freedom Ticket and Touristcard passes are available from the
Ticket Centre at the south end of Waverley Bridge and from
newsagents throughout the city)
Eastern Scottish city 'hopper' and commuter services 031-556 8464
(also the general number for the Coach Station, St. Andrew's Square)
Scottish Citylink 031-557 5717

USEFUL INFORMATION
FOR BUSINESS VISITORS

SECRETARIAL SERVICES

William Hodge, 20 York Place EH1	031-556 5660
Lindsay & MacLeod, 5 Blair Street EH1	031-226 3580
McNeill & Cadzow, 16a Ainslie Place EH3	031-225 8021
The Scribe, 23 Brougham Street EH3	031-228 4728
Typing Matters, 22 Chester Street EH3	031-220 1122
Wetherby Office Services, 93 High Street EH1	031-556 2548

CAR HIRE/ DRIVING

Traveline [recorded road information]	031-246 8021
Ansa International, Hilton International Hotel, Belford Road EH4	031-315 2868
Avis, 100 Dalry Road EH11	031-337 6363
Avis, Edinburgh Airport EH12	031-333 1866
Bradbury Car Rentals, 30a Brunswick Road EH7	031-556 1406
Budget, 116 Polwarth Gardens EH11	031-228 6088
Budget, Royal Scot Hotel, 111 Glasgow Road EH12	031-334 7740
Arnold Clark, 1/13 Lochrin Place EH3	031-228 4747
Condor Self Drive, 70-74 Morrison Street EH3	031-229 6333
Condor Self Drive, 180 Albert Street EH7	031-553 1166
Edinburgh Car & Van Rental, 70-74 Morrison Street EH3	031-229 8686
EuroDollar, Shrubhill Service Station EH7	031-555 0565
EuroDollar, Edinburgh Airport EH12	031-333 1922
Europcar UK, 24 East London Street EH7	031-661 1252
Europcar UK, Terminal Building EH12	031-333 2588
Guy Salmon Car Rentals, Caledonian Hotel, Princes Street EH1	031-226 7257
Hertz, 10 Picardy Place EH1	031-556 8311
Hertz, Edinburgh Airport EH12	031-333 1019
Hertz, Waverley Station EH1	031-557 5272
Kenning Motor Group, 37 Haddington Place EH7	031-557 5141
Lo Cost Car Hire, 1a Wardlaw Terrace EH11	031-313 2220
Mitchell Self Drive, 32 Torphichen Street EH3	031-229 5384
Practical Car & Van Rental, 13 Lauriston Gardens EH3	031-229 9399
Total Car & Van Rental, 45 Lochrin Place EH3	031-229 4548
Town & Country Car Rental UK, Queensway Hotel, EH4	031-343 3397
Turner Hire Drive, 16 Annandale Street EH7	031-557 0304
Woods Car Rental, c/o Crest Hotel, Queensferry Road EH4	031-343 2588

TAXIS

Bluebird Cars, 204 Great Junction Street EH6	031-553 6020
Capital Cabs, 28 North Bridge EH1	031-220 0404
Castle Cabs, 2 Torphichen Street EH3	031-228 2555
Central Radio Taxis, 163 Gilmore Place EH3	031-229 2468
City Cabs, 2 Atholl Place EH3	031-228 1211
Festival City Cars, 61a Queen Street EH2	031-220 3160
Radiocabs, 5 Upper Bow EH1	031-225 9000
Waverley Cabs, 14 Ashley Place EH6	031-557 5559

CHAUFFEUR CARS

Aristocars, 61 High Street EH1	031-557 8234
Bluebird Private Car Hire, 204 Great Junction Street EH6	031-553 6020
Countrywide Chauffeurs, 5 Silverknowes Avenue EH4	031-312 6338
Crown Cars, 55 Constitution Street EH6	031-554 6664
Edinburgh Airport Radio Cars, Edinburgh Airport EH12	031-339 5555
Edinburgh Fly Drive, 36 East Claremont Street EH7	031-556 5418
Executive Car Hire, Unit 24, 4 Comely Bank Row EH4	031-332 1211
Majestic Chauffeur Drive, 60 Montrose Terrace EH7	031-659 6482
Oz Cars, 9 Lower Gilmore Place EH3	031-228 6244

CUSTOMS

HM Customs and Excise:	Regional Head Office, 44 York Place EH1	031-556 2433
	Edinburgh Airport EH12	031-333 1044

BRITISH TELECOM SERVICES

Directory Enquiries	192
International Directory Enquiries	153
International Operator	155
Speaking Clock	123
International Telegrams / Telemessage	100

POSTAL SERVICES

Head Post Office, 2/4 Waterloo Place	031-550 8232

Other offices are marked on the maps
General opening times: Mon-Fri *9.00 – 17.30*
                           Sat *9.00 – 12.30*
                           (Many sub-post offices are closed at lunchtime)

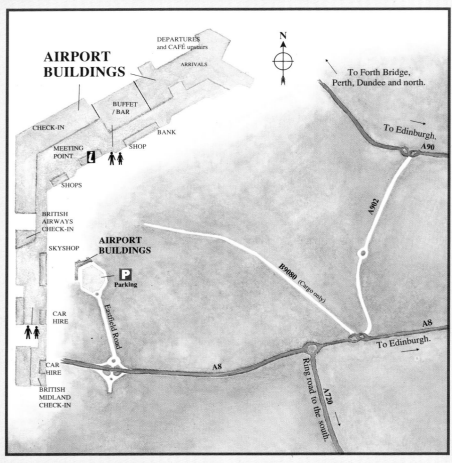

Edinburgh Airport Limited
Edinburgh EH12 9DN

TRAVEL TO AND FROM THE AIRPORT

Airline Bus
Links the airport with a terminus at Waverley Bridge in the City Centre. At peak times coaches run *every 30 minutes* (less frequent at other times). The journey takes about 25 minutes. Enquiries 031-226 5087 (031-554 4494 *after office hours).*

Taxis
Taxis are available outside the terminal. The journey to Edinburgh City Centre takes about 25 minutes and costs around £8.50. Tel: 031-344 3344

Private Car
From Edinburgh follow the A8 and proceed via the Maybury Roundabout towards Glasgow. Just before reaching the Royal Highland Showground, take the left-hand slip road and use the underpass beneath the dual carriageway to join the terminal approach road. The airport is clearly signposted.

Train
By Airline Bus to Waverley Bridge, which stands above the City's main railway station. From here there are train services to almost all regions of Scotland and England.

Car Hire
Several Car Hire companies operate within the terminal. See the Business section for details.

Air Taxis
Gleneagle Helicopter Services Ltd
031-339 2321

OTHER FACILITIES
Lost Property
Left Luggage
Emergency Medical Services
Nursery/Mothers' Room
Restaurants/Bars
Spectators' Gallery

USEFUL TELEPHONE NUMBERS
Information Desk	031-334 3136
Duty Manager	031-334 3323
Main switchboard	031-333 1000
HM Customs	031-334 3196
HM Immigration	031-334 3330
Police	031-334 3257
Restaurant	031-334 3119
Clydesdale Bank	031-333 3146

For general flight enquiries you should telephone the Information Desk.

Information kindly supplied by BAA.

BUSINESS DIRECTORY

MAJOR BUSINESSES IN EDINBURGH
Guide to using page / map references is at top of street index (page 78)

BANKS
Adam & Co	**40**	**F6**
22 Charlotte Square EH2	031-225 8484	
American Express	**41**	**F6**
139 Princes Street EH2	031-225 7881	
Bank of Scotland	**42**	**H6**
P.O.Box 5, The Mound EH2	031-442 7777	
British Linen Bank Ltd	**40**	**D6**
4 Melville Street EH3	031-453 1919	
Clydesdale Bank	**33**	**G5**
29 George Street EH2	031-225 4081	
Morgan Grenfell (Scotland)	**34**	**J5**
35 St Andrew Square EH2	031-556 6982	
Royal Bank of Scotland	**33**	**G5**
14 George Street EH2	031-225 7023	
Royal Bank of Scotland	**41**	**F6**
142 Princes Street EH2	031-556 8555	
Royal Bank of Scotland	**34**	**J5**
36 St Andrew Square EH2	031-556 8555	
TSB Scotland	**33**	**G5**
P.O.Box 177, 120 George Street EH2	031-225 4555	

LEGAL: SOLICITORS and others
Brodies	**40**	**D7**
15 Atholl Crescent EH3	031-228 3777	
Dundas & Wilson	**40**	**F6**
25 Charlotte Square EH2	031-225 1234	
Maclay Murray & Spens	**32**	**E5**
3 Glenfinlas Street EH3	031-226 5196	
Morton, Fraser & Milligan	**35**	**K4**
15 & 19 York Place EH1	031-556 8444	
Shepherd & Wedderburn	**40**	**F6**
16 Charlotte Square EH2	031-225 8585	

SURVEYORS and ESTATE AGENTS
Sir Alexander Gibb & Partners	**31**	**C4**
30 Queensferry Road EH4	031-315 6207	
Bernard Thorpe	**33**	**G5**
46A George Street EH2	031-226 4484	
Jones Lang Wootton	**33**	**F5**
10 Castle Street EH2	031-225 8344	

BUSINESS and FINANCIAL SERVICES
3i	**40**	**F6**
8 Charlotte Square EH2	031-226 7092	
Baillie Marshall	**40**	**E6**
8 Randolph Place EH3	031-226 3794	
A C Bennett & Robertsons	**39**	**D6**
16 Walker Street EH3	031-225 4001	
B.D.O. Binder Hamlyn	**39**	**D7**
11 Manor Place EH3	031-225 6366	
Collins Halden (Scotland)	**39**	**D6**
9 Melville Crescent EH3	031-226 7699	
Dawson International	**40**	**F6**
9 Charlotte Square EH2	031-220 1919	
Fuller Peiser	**39**	**D6**
21 Walker Street EH3	031-225 9816	
The L.A.S. Group	**33**	**G5**
10 George Street EH2	031-225 8494	
P A Consulting Group	**34**	**H5**
80 Hanover Street EH2	031-225 4481	
PIEDA	**39**	**C6**
10 Chester Street EH1	031-225 5737	

Price Waterhouse	**39**	**D6**
28 Drumsheugh Gardens EH3	031-225 4242	
Royal Incorporation of Architects	**40**	**E7**
15 Rutland Square EH1	031-229 7205	
Ryden	**34**	**H5**
71 Hanover Street EH2	031-225 6612	
Scottish Industrial & Trade Exhibitions	**40**	**F6**
8A Charlotte Square EH2	031-225 5486	

INDUSTRIAL
Anderson Brown & Co	**29**	**P2**
St Andrews Steelworks, Albion Road EH7	031-661 7974	
Balfour Beatty Construction	**30**	**B5**
23 Ravelston Terrace EH4	031-332 9411	
Blyth & Blyth Group	**33**	**G5**
135 George Street EH2	031-225 6283	
Brown Brothers & Co	**26**	**K27**
144 Broughton Road EH7	031-556 2440	
Carlyle Scotland	**54**	**L26**
1c Pilrig Street EH6	031-553 2174	
Charles Henshaw & Sons		Off map
Russell Road EH11	031-337 4204	
Craig & Rose	**35**	**L4**
172 Leith Walk EH6	031-554 1131	
GEC Ferranti Defence Systems		Off map
Crewe Toll EH5	031-332 2411	
T. Harley Haddow & Partners	**40**	**D7**
8 Coates Crescent EH3	031-226 3331	
Leith Glazing Co	**55**	**P23**
93 Giles Street EH6	031-553 1471	
Alexander Mather & Son	**25**	**F2**
9 West Silvermills Lane EH3	031-556 7475	
T. Miller & Co	**28**	**M3**
Foundry London Road EH7	031-661 1371	
Morrison Construction Group	**40**	**D7**
12 Atholl Crescent EH3	031-228 4188	
R.O.C.C. Computers	**31**	**C4**
30 Queensferry Road EH4	031-332 1316	
Trafalgar House Offshore & Structural	**39**	**D6**
1 Melville Crescent EH3	031-226 2470	
Unisys	**40**	**F6**
13 Charlotte Square EH2	031-226 3537	
Waverley Cameron	**43**	**K7**
23 Blair Street EH1	031-220 2828	
Wolfson Microelectronics	**52**	**M10**
20 Bernard Terrace EH8	031-667 9386	

PUBLISHING
Bartholomew	**56**	**M12**
12 Duncan Street EH9	031-667 9341	
Churchill Livingstone	**35**	**L4**
1-3 Baxter Place, Leith Walk EH1	031-556 2424	
Edinburgh University Press	**51**	**K9**
22 George Square EH8	031-667 1011	
Johnston Press	**39**	**D7**
53 Manor Place EH3	031-225 3361	
The Scotsman Publications	**43**	**K6**
20 North Bridge EH1	031-225 2468	
Scottish Newspaper Publishers Association	**40**	**C7**
48 Palmerston Place EH12	031-220 4353	

FOOD INDUSTRY
Christian Salveson	**23**	**C1**
50 East Fettes Avenue EH4	031-552 7101	
Crawfords	**55**	**Q23**
19 Elbe Street EH6	031-554 6651	
John Crabbie & Co	**55**	**M23**
108 Great Junction Street EH6	031-554 5336	
Scottish Agricultural Industries	**30**	**B5**
25 Ravelston Terrace EH4	031-332 2481	
William Muir (Bond 9)	**55**	**Q23**
42 Elbe Street EH6	031-554 4355	

DISTILLERS and BREWERS

MacDonald Martin Distilleries	**55**	**M22**
186 Commercial Street EH6	031-554 4477	
Scottish & Newcastle Breweries	**45**	**N6**
111 Holyrood Road EH8	031-556 2591	
United Malt & Grain Distillers	**31**	**C4**
603 Queensferry Road EH4	031-339 4042	

RETAIL

John Menzies	**42**	**G5**
Hanover Buildings, Rose Street EH2	031-225 8555	

LEISURE

Scottish Tourist Board	**30**	**B5**
23 Ravelston Terrace EH4	031-332 2433	

P.R., ADVERTISING and MEDIA

Applied Learning	**35**	**K4**
22 York Place EH1	031-557 9191	
Charles Barker Scotland	**40**	**E7**
18 Rutland Square EH1	031-229 7493	
The Berlitz School of Languages	**33**	**G5**
24/26 Frederick Street EH2	031-226 7198	
Hall Advertising	**39**	**D6**
24 Drumsheugh Gardens EH3	031-225 1211	

OTHER BUSINESSES

Anchor Line	**55**	**Q24**
11 John's Place EH6	031-554 4466	
Ben Line Group	**44**	**L6**
33 St Mary's Street EH1	031-557 2323	
British Telecom (East Scotland) District	**40**	**E7**
19a Canning Street EH3	031-229 2525	
Scottish Transport Group	**33**	**F5**
114-116 George Street EH2	031-226 7491	

INSURANCE and LIFE ASSURANCE

Alexander Stenhouse UK	**33**	**G5**
78/80 George Street EH2	031-226 2515	
Allied Dunbar	**31**	**B4**
30 Queensferry Road EH4	031-315 2555	
Clerical, Medical & General Life Ass. Soc.	**34**	**J5**
5 St Andrew Square EH2	031-557 0826	
Colonial Mutual Life Assurance Society	**40**	**E6**
4 Charlotte Lane EH2	031-226 2636	
Commercial Union	**33**	**G5**
26 George Street EH2	031-225 2500	
Confederation Life Ass. Co. (of Canada)	**31**	**C4**
30 Queensferry Road EH4	031-315 2605	
Cornhill Insurance	**34**	**H5**
80 Hanover Street EH2	031-226 5611	
Dominion Insurance Co	**31**	**C4**
30 Queensferry Road EH4	031-343 2686	
Eagle Star Insurance Co	**34**	**J5**
25 St Andrew Square EH2	031-556 9971	
Equity & Law Life Assurance Society	**33**	**F5**
110 George Street EH2	031-225 6054	
Friends Provident Life Office	**33**	**G5**
80 George Street EH2	031-226 4513	
FS Assurance	**40**	**E6**
6 Hope Street EH2	031-226 4174	
General Accident Fire & Life Ass. Corp.	**46**	**A8**
1 Osborne Terrace EH12	031-337 2454	
GRE (UK)	**34**	**J5**
13 St Andrew Square EH2	031-225 5871	
Hill Samuel Investment Services	**33**	**H5**
18 George Street EH2	031-225 7595	
Ivory & Sime	**40**	**F6**
1 Charlotte Square EH2	031-225 1357	
Legal & General Assurance Society	**40**	**F6**
23 Charlotte Square EH2	031-225 2666	

Life Association of Scotland	**33**	**H15**
10 George Street EH2	031-225 8494	
MGM Assurance	**34**	**H5**
80 Hanover Street EH2	031-226 6121	
National Vulcan Engineering Ins. Group	**33**	**G5**
42 Frederick Street EH2	031-225 5279	
Norwich Union Insurance Group	**34**	**J5**
32-34 St Andrew Square EH2	031-556 2581	
Provincial Insurance	**40**	**F8**
2 Festival Square EH3	031-228 4151	
Quayle Munro	**40**	**F6**
42 Charlotte Square EH2	031-226 4421	
Royal Insurance UK	**33**	**F5**
107 George Street EH2	031-225 1221	
Scottish Amicable Life Assurance	**33**	**F5**
54 Castle Street EH2	031-225 41 ¦4	
Scottish Equitable Life Assurance Soc.	**34**	**J5**
28 St Andrew Square EH2	031-556 9101	
Scottish Life Assurance Company	**34**	**J5**
19 St Andrew Square EH2	031-225 2211	
Scottish Provident Institution	**34**	**J5**
6 St Andrew Square EH2	031-556 9181	
Scottish Widows' Fund & Life Ass. Soc.	**56**	**N11**
15 Dalkeith Road EH16	031-655 6000	
Standard Life Assurance Co.	**33**	**G5**
3 George Street EH2	031-225 2552	
Sun Alliance Insurance Group	**33**	**G5**
68 George Street EH2	031-226 7361	
Sun Life Assurance Co. of Canada	**40**	**E7**
67 Shandwick Place EH2	031-228 3003	
Sun Life Assurance Society	**33**	**F5**
22 Castle Street EH2	031-225 7498	
Towry Law & Co	**40**	**D6**
30 Melville Street EH3	031-557 2100	
UK Provident	**33**	**G5**
80 George Street EH2	031-226 4513	

JUSTICIARY

Crown Office	**37**	**N4**
5/7 Regent Road EH7	031-556 3800	
High Court of Justiciary		Off map
2 Crewe Toll EH5	031-225 2595	
Scottish Courts Administration	**36**	**H7**
26 Royal Terrace EH7	031-556 0755	

SCOTTISH OFFICE

Crown Office	**37**	**N4**
5/7 Regent Road EH7	031-556 3800	
Land Tribunal for Scotland	**40**	**C7**
1 Grosvenor Crescent EH12	031-225 7996	
Mental Welfare Commission for Scotland	**40**	**D6**
22 Melville Street EH3	031-225 7034	
New St Andrew's House	**35**	**K4**
St James Centre EH1	031-556 8400	
St Andrew's House	**36**	**L5**
Regent Road EH1	031-556 8400	
Scottish Development Department	**35**	**K4**
New St Andrew's Hse, St James Ctr. EH1	031-556 8400	
Scottish Education Department	**43**	**L6**
43 Jeffrey Street EH1	031-556 8400	

PRIVATE INVESTIGATORS

Brickell (International) Investigations	**26**	**H3**
82 Great King Street EH3	031-557 0354	
Robert Good & Co	**40**	**E7**
12 Rutland Square EH1	031-228 2281	
Grant & McMurtrie	**39**	**B8**
3 Grosvenor Gardens EH12	031-337 7252	
Thomas C. Gray	**42**	**J7**
1 India Buildings EH1	031-226 5931	
Malcolm W. Thompson	**33**	**G4**
21 Heriot Row EH3	031-225 6511	

SHOPS, THEATRES, HOTELS, SIGHTS, PUBS & PLACES TO EAT

uide to using page / map references is at top of street index (page 78)

RESTAURANTS

Bell's Diner — 16 F3
7 St Stephen Street EH3 — 031-225 0257
Bianco's — 40 E6
9-11 Hope Street EH2 — 031-226 2047
Bib & Tucker — 24 E3
2 Deanhaugh Street EH4 — 031-332 1469
Blah! Blah! — 47 C9
63 Dalry Road EH11 — 031-313 2139
Blue Parrot — 16 F3
49 St Stephen Street EH3 — 031-225 2941
Brasserie St Jacques (in St James Hotel) — 35 K5
107 Leith Street EH1 — 031-556 0111
Buntoms — 34 H3
9-13 Nelson Street EH3 — 031-557 4344
Ca Va — 43 K6
133 High Street EH1 — 031-556 3276
Café Coste — 43 K7
3 Cowgate EH1 — 031-557 6849
Café Royal — 15 J5
17 West Register Street EH2 — 031-556 4124
Caprice — 55 N27
327 Leith Walk EH6 — 031-554 1279
Chambertin Restaurant — 15 H5
19-21 George Street EH2 — 031-225 1251
Cibo — 15 H4
109 Hanover Street EH2 — 031-220 4854
PJ Clarkes — 32 F5
80 Queen Street EH2 — 031-220 2052
Concorde Fish Bar — 49 F9
49 Home Street EH3 — 031-228 1182
Dragon's Castle — 14 F6
21 Castle Street EH2 — 031-225 7327
Dragon's Pearl — 35 L3
20 Union Place EH1 — 031-556 4547
Duncan's Land — 32 E3
8 Gloucester Street EH3 — 031-225 1037
Fat Sams — 48 E9
58 Fountainbridge EH3 — 031-228 3111
Gennaro — 13 H7
64 Grassmarket EH1 — 031-226 3706
Great Wall — 41 F8
105-109 Lothian Road EH3 — 031-229 7747
Hamiltons — 16 F3
18 Hamilton Place EH3 — 031-226 4199
Henderson's — 15 H5
94 Hanover Street EH2 — 031-225 2131
Howie's — 52 M9
75 St Leonard's Street EH8 — 031-668 2917
Indian Cavalry Club — 40 D7
3 Atholl Place EH3 — 031-228 3282
Kalpna — 52 L9
2-3 St Patrick Square EH8 — 031-667 9890
Keepers — 34 H4
13B Dundas Street EH3 — 031-556 5707
Kelly's — 44 L8
46 West Richmond Street EH8 — 031-668 3847
Khushi — 27 J3
32c Broughton Street EH1 — 031-556 8092
Kohinoor — 43 L8
14a Nicolson Street EH8 — 031-556 6583
Kweilin — 34 H4
19-21 Dundas Street EH3 — 031-556 1752
L'Aperitif — 41 F8
Grindlay Street EH3 — 031-229 8663
L'Auberge — 44 L7
58 St Mary's Street EH1 — 031-556 5888
La Lanterna — 15 H5
83 Hanover Street EH2 — 031-226 3090
Lake Van Monastery in Exile — 37 N5
55 Abbeyhill EH8 — 031-557 0435
Lancers — 16 F3
5 Hamilton Place EH3 — 031-332 3444
Le Bagatelle — 49 G9
22a Brougham Place EH3 — 031-229 0869
Le Bon Fondue — 55 P22
30 Sandport Street EH6 — 031-554 2921
Le Sept — 43 K7
7 Old Fishmarket Close EH1 — 031-225 5428
Loon Fung — 41 F8
2 Grindlay Street EH3 — 031-229 5757

Loon Fung — 25 G1
2 Warriston Place EH3 — 031-556 1781
Lune Town — 39 D7
38 William Street EH3 — 031-220 1688
Ma Cuisine — 16 F3
42 St Stephen Street EH3 — 031-226 5877
Mammas — 13 H7
30 Grassmarket EH1 — 031-225 6464
Marché Noir — 25 G2
2-4 Eyre Place EH3 — 031-558 1608
Marrakech — 26 J2
30 London Street EH3 — 031-556 7293
Martin's — 16 G5
70 Rose Street North Lane EH2 — 031-225 3106
Mary Rose Bistro — 15 H4
112 Hanover Street EH2 — 031-225 2022
Mc Kirdy's — 55 Q23
43 Assembly Street EH6 — 031-553 6363
Modica's — 15 G6
17A Frederick Street EH2 — 031-225 5697
Mr V's — 40 E6
7 Charlotte Lane EH2 — 031-220 0176
Negociants — 43 K8
45-47 Lothian Street EH1 — 031-225 6313
Omar Khayyam — 39 C8
1 Grosvenor Street EH12 — 031-225 2481
Orchid Lodge — 15 G6
15A Castle Street EH2 — 031-226 2505
Pachuko Cantina — 48 D8
3 Grove Street EH3 — 031-228 1345
Pancake Place — 40 E7
35 Shandwick Place EH2 — 031-228 6322
Patio Restaurant — 15 H5
87 Hanover Street EH2 — 031-226 3653
Phillipine Island — 27 K3
36 Broughton Street EH1 — 031-556 8240
Pierre Victoire — 35 K3
8 Union Street EH1 — 031-557 8451
Pierre Victoire — 13 J7
10 Victoria Street EH1 — 031-225 1721
Pingon — 24 E3
26-32 Deanhaugh Street EH4 — 031-332 3621
Pukhet Penang — 14 F6
176 Rose Street EH2 — 031-220 0059
Raffaeli — 40 E6
10 Randolph Place EH3 — 031-225 6060
The Raj — 55 P23
89/91a Henderson Street EH6 — 031-553 3980
Rendezvous — 24 E3
24 Deanhaugh Street EH4 — 031-332 4476
Rock Bottom — 40 E6
9 Shandwick Place EH2 — 031-228 6006
Round Table — 43 K6
31 Jeffrey Street EH1 — 031-557 3032
Shamiana — 49 G9
14 Brougham Street EH3 — 031-229 5578
Shanaz — 14 G6
129a Rose Street EH2 — 031-226 2862
Shore — 55 P22
3 Shore, The EH6 — 031-553 5080
Skippers Bistro — 55 P22
1a Dock Place EH6 — 031-554 1018
Tinelli — 29 P2
139 Easter Road EH7 — 031-652 1932
Traverse Café — 13 J7
112 West Bow EH1 — 031-226 2633
Umberto's — 34 J3
29 Dublin Street EH1 — 031-556 2231
Verandha Tandoori — 47 C8
17 Dalry Road EH11 — 031-337 5828
Vintner's Room — 55 P23
87 Giles Street EH6 — 031-554 6767
Viva Mexico — 43 K6
10 Cockburn Street EH1 — 031-226 5145
Waterfront Wine Bar — 55 P22
1c Dock Place EH6 — 031-554 7427
The World — 15 G5
55 Thistle Street EH2 — 031-225 3275
Yee Kiang — 55 N27
42 Dalmeny Street EH6 — 031-554 5833

CAFÉS Coffees, take-outs & light meals

Baker's Oven — 14 G6
6 Frederick Street EH2 — 031-220 1044
Bar Napoli — 15 H5
75 Hanover Street EH2 — 031-225 2600
Blue Moon Café — 27 J3
60 Broughton Street EH1 — 031-556 2788
Bonnington's — 52 L10
75 Clerk Street EH8 — 031-668 1855

Breadwinner
20 Bruntsfield Place EH10 — 49 F10 — 031-229 7247
Burger King
118 Princes Street EH2 — 14 F6 — 031-220 1644
Café
F6 Lower Level,Waverley Shopping Centre EH1 — 17 WL — 031-557 5616
Café Saint Honore
34 Thistle Street EH2 — 15 G5 — 031-226 2211
Charlie McNair's
30 Forrest Road EH1 — 43 J8 — 031-226 6434
Chopstick Express
F8 Lower Level,Waverley Shopping Centre EH1 — 17 WL — 031-557 3217
Circles
324 Lawnmarket EH1 — 42 J7 — 031-225 9505
City Café
19 Blair Street EH1 — 43 K7 — 031-220 0125
Clarinda's
68 Canongate EH8 — 45 N6 — 031-557 1888
Cody's
F9 Lower Level,Waverley Shopping Centre EH1 — 17 WL — 031-556 4768
Coffee Stop
L15 Lower Level,Waverley Shopping Centre EH1 — 17 WL — 031-557 3079
Cornerstone (under St John's Church)
Princes Street EH2 — 40 F6 — 031-229 0212
Di Placido
36 High Street EH1 — 43 L6 — 031-557 2286
Di's Deli
64 Clerk Street EH8 — 52 L10 — 031-668 4223
Edinburgh Delicacies Centre
7 Barony Street EH3 — 27 J3 — 031-556 7676
Edinburgh Wine Bar
110 Hanover Street EH2 — 15 H5 — 031-220 1208
Eggs and Things
F1 Lower Level,Waverley Shopping Centre EH1 — 17 WL — 031-556 3655
Eliot's
5a William Street EH3 — 40 D6 — 031-226 6715
Fleur's
52 Shore, The EH6 — 55 P23 — 031-554 8841
Florentin
25a Thistle Street EH2 — 15 H5 — 031-225 3103
Gallery of Modern Art Café
Belford Road EH4 — 38 A6 — 031-556 8921
Gerry's
71 Rose Street EH2 — 15 G5 — 031-225 8012
Grange Deli
8 Grange Loan EH9 — 56 M12 — 031-668 2120
Helios Fountain
7 Grassmarket EH1 — 13 H8 — 031-229 7884
Jo-Ann's Café
248 Dalry Road EH11 — 46 A10 — 031-337 0869
Kinnells (Café)
36 Victoria Street EH1 — 13 J7 — 031-220 1150
Kinnells (Deli)
88-92 West Bow EH1 — 13 J7 — 031-226 7478
Kinnells House
36 Victoria Street EH1 — 13 H7 — 031-220 1150
Le Bistro
11 William Street EH3 — 40 D7 — 031-225 3713
Lilligs Café
30 Victoria Street EH1 — 13 J7 — 031-225 7635
Madogs
38 George Street EH2 — 15 H5 — 031-225 3408
Mano's Deli
28 Lochrin Buildings EH3 — 49 F10 — 031-229 7771
Maxies Bistro
32 West Nicolson Street EH8 — 51 L9 — 031-667 0845
McDonalds
137 Princes Street EH2 — 14 F6 — 031-226 3872
Miro
184 Rose Street EH2 — F6 — 031-222 4376
Mr Boni
4 Lochrin Buildings EH3 — 49 F10 — 031-229 0914
Mr Doughnut's Bakery
43 Leven Street EH3 — 52 M9 — 031-228 2996
Mrs Beeton's
42 Broughton Street EH1 — 27 J3 — 031-557 2726
Oven Fresh Bakeries
147 Morrison Street EH3 — 40 D8 — 031-229 6470
Picnic Basket
31 West Nicolson Street EH8 — 51 K9 — 031-667 9392
Quality Foods
27 Bread Street EH3 — 41 F8 — 031-229 4343
Queen's Hall Café
South Clerk Street EH8 — 52 M10 — 031-668 3456
St Elmo's
7 Victoria Street EH1 — 13 J7 — 031-226 5260
Sauceboat
1 Bernard Street EH6 — 55 Q23 — 031-554 3628
Scots Pantry
F3 Lower Level,Waverley Shopping Centre EH1 — 17 WL — 031-557 5130

Sea Fresh
 — 17 — 031- ?
F5 Lower Level,Waverley Shopping Centre EH1 — 031-556 4(
Seeds Co-Op
53 West Nicolson Street EH8 — 51 — 031-667 86
Spud-U-Like
F4 Lower Level,Waverley Shopping Centre EH1 — 17 W — 031-557 1?
Sunflower Country Kitchen
4-8 South Charlotte Street EH2 — 14 — 031-220 1?
Swop Shop
224 Dalry Road EH11 — 46 A — 031-337 13
Three Coins
19 Home Street EH3 — 49 — 031-229 77
Trader Vic's
4 Victoria Street EH1 — 13 — 031-225 65
Umberto's Deli
27 Dublin Street EH1 — 34 — 031-556 2)
Valvona & Crolla
19 Elm Row EH7 — 28 — 031-556 6(
Wimpy
10 Princes Street EH2 — 15 — 031-557 4?
Wolfit's Deli
23 Henderson Row EH3 — 25 — 031-556 58

PUBS

Auld Hundred
100 Rose Street EH2 — 15 — 031-225 1?
Baillie
2 St Stephen Street EH3 — 16 — 031-225 46
Bannerman's
55 Niddry Street EH1 — 43 — 031-556 32
Barony Bar
81 Broughton Street EH1 — 27 — 031-557 05
Beau Brummel
99 Hanover Street EH2 — 34 — 031-225 46
Beehive Inn
18-20 Grassmarket EH1 — 13 — 031-225 71
Bernards
27 Bernard Street EH6 — 55 Q — 031-554 52
Black Bo's
57 Blackfriars Street EH1 — 43 — 031-557 61
Black Bull
12 Grassmarket EH1 — 13 — 031-225 66
Blue Blanket
232 Canongate EH8 — 44 — 031-556 44
Boundary Bar
379 Leith Walk EH7 — 28 — 031-554 22
Bristo Bar
41 Lothian Street EH1 — 43 — 031-225 97
Café Biarritz
61 Frederick Street EH2 — 15 — 031-225 52
Candlemakers Arms
5 Cowgatehead EH1 — 13 — 031-220 23
Carldon Lounge
142 Duke Street EH6 — 55 Q — 031-554 38
Cellar No.1 Wine Bar
1 Chambers Street EH1 — 43 — 031-220 42
Chesterfield's
3a Royal Terrace EH7 — 36 — 031-556 69
Claret Jug
34 Great King Street EH3 — 26 — 031-557 38
Cottars
21 Rose Street EH2 — 15 — 031-225 56
Deacon Brodie's Tavern
435 Lawnmarket EH1 — 42 — 031-225 65
Ensign Ewart
521 Lawnmarket EH1 — 42 — 031-225 74
Fiddlers Arms
9-11 Grassmarket EH1 — 13 — 031-229 26
Forrest Hill (Sandy Bell's)
25 Forrest Road EH1 — 42 — 031-225 11
Green Tree
182-184 Cowgate EH1 — 43 — 031-225 12
Guildford Arms
1 West Register Street EH2 — 15 — 031-556 43
Hanover Pub
88-90 Hanover Street EH2 — 15 — 031-225 22
Joe's Garage
21 Lothian Road EH1 — 40 — 031-228 34
Jolly Judge
7 James's Court EH1 — 42 — 031-225 26
Kay's Bar
39 Jamaica Street EH3 — 33 — 031-225 15
Kenilworth
152-154 Rose Street EH2 — 14 — 031-225 8)
L'Odeon
49-50 George IV Bridge EH1 — 43 — 031-220 49
Last Drop
74 Grassmarket EH1 — 13 — 031-225 48
Laughing Duck
24 Howe Street EH3 — 33 — 031-225 67

Mather	**35**	**K3**
25 Broughton Street EH1	031-556 6754	
Moncrieffs	**15**	**G5**
39 Thistle Street EH2	031-225 6191	
Northern Bar	**25**	**G1**
1 Howard Place EH3	031-556 1558	
Oblomov	**42**	**J6**
11-13 North Bank Street EH1	031-220 0054	
Oddfellows	**43**	**J8**
14 Forrest Road EH1	031-220 1816	
Original Dock Tavern	**55**	**P22**
3-4 Dock Place EH6	031-554 7395	
Pear Tree	**51**	**L9**
38 West Nicolson Street EH8	031-667 7796	
Pier's Point	**55**	**P22**
1 Shore, The EH6	031-554 5666	
Preservation Hall	**13**	**J7**
9 Victoria Street EH1	031-226 3816	
Rose & Crown	**14**	**F6**
170 Rose Street EH2	031-225 4039	
St Vincent	**25**	**F3**
9 St Vincent Street EH3	031-225 7447	
Scotts	**14**	**F6**
202 Rose Street EH2	031-225 7401	
Shambles	**24**	**E3**
47 Deanhaugh Street EH4	031-332 5328	
Stockbridge Bar	**16**	**F3**
44 St Stephen Street EH3	031-220 3774	
Tilted Wig	**26**	**H3**
1-3 Cumberland Street EH3	031-556 9409	
Whigham's Wine Cellar	**40**	**E6**
13 Hope Street EH2	031-225 9717	
White Hart Inn	**13**	**H7**
34 Grassmarket EH1	031-226 2688	
Wine Glass	**56**	**M11**
1-5 Newington Road EH9	031-667 6868	

CINEMAS

Cameo	**49**	**F9**
38 Home Street EH3	031-228 4141	
Cannon Centre	**40**	**F8**
120 Lothian Road EH3	031-229 3030 (229 1638 Recorded Message)	
Filmhouse	**40**	**F8**
88 Lothian Road EH3	031-228 2688	
Odeon Film Theatre	**52**	**L10**
7 Clerk Street EH8	031-667 7331	

THEATRE and FRINGE / FESTIVAL VENUES

Acoustic Music Centre (E.U.Union)	**43**	**K7**
16 Chambers Street EH1	031-220 2468	
Assembly Rooms	**15**	**H5**
54 George Street EH2	031-226 2428	
Bedlam Theatre	**43**	**J8**
2 Forrest Road EH1	031-225 9873	
Bookfare	**13**	**J7**
8 Victoria Street EH1	031-225 9237	
Central Hall	**49**	**F9**
3 West Tollcross EH3	031-229 7937	
Comedy Room	**35**	**K3**
2 Picardy Place EH1	031-556 0499	
Edinburgh College of Art	**49**	**G8**
74 Lauriston Place EH3	031-229 9311	
Festival Club	**43**	**K7**
9-15 Chambers Street EH1	031-225 8283	
Fringe Club	**43**	**K8**
Bristo Square EH8	031-226 5257	
George Square Theatre	**51**	**K9**
George Square EH8	031-667 1011	
Gilded Balloon	**43**	**K7**
233 Cowgate EH1	031-225 4463	
Institut Français D'Ecosse	**32**	**D5**
13 Randolph Crescent EH3	031-225 5366	
King's Theatre	**49**	**G10**
2 Leven Street EH3	031-229 1201	
Moray House Theatre	**10**	**M6**
37 Holyrood Park Road EH16	031-556 8455	
Netherbow Art Centre	**43**	**L6**
43 High Street EH1	031-556 9579	
Old St Paul's Church & Hall	**43**	**K6**
Jeffrey Street EH1	-	
Overseas House	**14**	**G6**
100 Princes Street EH2	031-225 5105	
Pharmaceutical Society	**35**	**K4**
36 York Place EH1	031-556 4386	
Playhouse Theatre	**35**	**L4**
18-21 Greenside Place EH1	031-557 2590	
Pleasance Theatre	**44**	**L7**
60 Pleasance EH8	031-556 6550	
Queen's Hall	**52**	**M10**
Clerk Street EH8	031-668 3456	

Ross Open Air Theatre	**42**	**G6**
Princes Street EH2	-	
Royal College of Physicians	**34**	**H4**
9 Queen Street EH2	031-225 7231	
Royal Lyceum Theatre (back of Usher Hall)	**41**	**F7**
Grindlay Street EH3	031-229 9697	
Royal Scots Club	**34**	**H4**
30 Abercromby Place EH3	031-556 4270	
St Andrew & St George	**35**	**J5**
George Street EH2	031-225 3847	
St Andrew's Hall	**27**	**J2**
Cochran Terrace EH12	-	
St Ann's Community Centre	**44**	**L7**
South Gray's Close EH1	031-557 0469	
St Bernard's	**24**	**F2**
Saxe Coburg Street EH3	031-332 0122	
St Cecilia's Hall	**43**	**K7**
Niddry Street EH1	031-667 1011	
St Columba's by the Castle	**42**	**H7**
Johnston Terrace EH1	031-220 1410	
St Mark's Unitarian Church	**41**	**F7**
Castle Terrace EH1	031-667 4360	
St Philip's Church & Hall	**52**	**M10**
Lutton Place EH8	-	
St Stephen's Church	**24**	**F3**
St Stephen Street EH3	-	
Salvation Army Hall	**44**	**L8**
5 East Adam Street EH8	031-662 4441	
South Bridge Centre	**43**	**L7**
Infirmary Street EH1	-	
Southside Community Centre "Southside International"	**52**	**L9**
117 Nicolson Street EH8	031-667 7365	
Student Centre	**51**	**K8**
5 Bristo Square EH8	031-667 0214	
Theatre West End	**40**	**F6**
40 Princes Street EH2	031-447 5685	
Theatre Workshop	**16**	**F3**
34 Hamilton Place EH3	031-225 7942	
Traverse Theatre	**13**	**J7**
112 West Bow EH1	031-226 2633	
Usher Hall	**41**	**F7**
Lothian Road EH1	031-228 1155	
Wee Red Bar	**50**	**H8**
74 Lauriston Place EH3	031-229 9311	
West & Wilde Bookshop	**34**	**H3**
25a Dundas Street EH3	031-556 0079	

ART GALLERIES

369 Gallery	**43**	**K7**
233 Cowgate EH1	031-225 3013	
Ash Gallery	**44**	**M6**
156 Canongate EH8	031-556 2160	
Bourne Fine Art	**33**	**G4**
4 Dundas Street EH3	031-557 4050	
Calton Gallery	**36**	**M4**
10 Royal Terrace EH7	031-556 1010	
Central Library	**42**	**J7**
3-9 George IV Bridge EH1	031-225 5584	
City Art Centre	**43**	**J6**
2 Market Street EH7	031-225 2424	
Daniel Shackleton	**34**	**H4**
17 Dundas Street EH3	031-557 1115	
Richard Demarco	**43**	**L7**
17-21 Blackfriars Street EH1	031-557 0707	
Dublin Street Studio	**26**	**J3**
73 Dublin Street EH3	031-557 5259	
Edinburgh College of Art	**49**	**G8**
74 Lauriston Place EH3	031-229 9311	
Fidelo	**25**	**G3**
49 Cumberland Street EH3	031-557 2444	
Fine Art Gallery	**34**	**H3**
41 Dundas Street EH3	031-557 4569	
Fine Art Society	**14**	**F5**
137 George Street EH2	031-220 6370	
Flying Colours	**39**	**D7**
35 William Street EH3	031-225 6776	
Forrest McKay	**33**	**F4**
38 Howe Street EH3	031-226 2589	
Bob Fraser Gallery	**17**	**WL**
L2a Lower Level, Waverley Shopping Centre EH1	031-557 3875	
Fruitmarket Gallery	**43**	**K6**
29 Market Street EH7	031-225 2383	
Galerie Mirages	**24**	**D2**
46a Raeburn Place EH4	031-315 2603	
Hanover Fine Arts	**33**	**G4**
22a Dundas Street EH3	031-556 2181	
Hillside Gallery	**28**	**M3**
6 Hillside Street EH7	031-556 6440	
Inverleith House		**RBG**
20a Inverleith Row EH3	031-552 7171	

Emma Roy	35	K5
31/33 Leith Street EH1	031-557 2875	
Eurosport	17	WL
L19 Lower Level,Waverley Shopping Centre EH1	031-556 6468	
Evans	15	J5
10-15 Princes Street EH2	031-557 0886	
Eyecatchers	13	H7
84 West Bow EH1	031-226 2532	
Flamingo Dress Hire	33	G4
3 Dundas Street EH3	031-226 3669	
Flip	43	K7
60-62 South Bridge EH1	031-556 4966	
Gieves & Hawkes	15	H5
48 George Street EH2	031-225 7456	
Gleneagles	17	WU
U27 Upper Level, Waverley Shopping Centre EH1	031-557 1777	
Hand in Hand	16	F3
3 North West Circus Place EH3	031-226 3598	
Head Gear	17	WU
Upper Level, Waverley Shopping Centre EH1		
High & Mighty	14	F6
4 Castle Street EH2	031-226 6254	
Highland Home Industries	17	WU
U5 Upper Level, Waverley Shopping Centre EH1	031-556 3088	
Hoi Polloi	14	G6
118/120 Rose Street EH2	031-225 2851	
Hyne & Eames	44	L6
299 Canongate EH8	031-557 4056	
India Shop	13	H7
32 Victoria Street EH1	031-220 4080	
Jaeger	15	H6
119a Princes Street EH2	031-225 8811	
James Pringle Woollen Mill	55	M24
70-74 Bangor Road EH6	031-553 5161	
Jane Davidson	15	G5
52 Thistle Street EH2	031-225 3280	
June Johnston Shoes	40	E6
5 William Street EH3	031-225 3663	
Jolly Holly	15	G5
60 Thistle Street EH2	031-226 4540	
Kiltmaker	15	J5
45 Princes Street EH2	031-556 6330	
Knitwear Gallery	17	WL
L21b Lower Level,Waverley Shopping Centre EH1	031-556 0472	
La Jolie Madame	39	D7
28 William Street EH3	031-225 7581	
Laura Ashley	14	G5
90 George Street EH2	031-225 1121	
Laura Ashley	14	F6
126 Princes Street EH2	031-225 1218	
Leisure & Pleasure	17	WL
L21a Lower Level,Waverley Shopping Centre EH1	031-556 7849	
Long Tall Sally	13	J7
1 Victoria Street EH1	031-225 8330	
Mackenzie	13	J7
26 Victoria Street EH1	031-220 0089	
Andrea Mackie	39	D7
45 William Street EH3	031-220 0320	
Marni	17	WU
U22 Upper Level, Waverley Shopping Centre EH1	031-556 2411	
McMillen	46	B10
176 Dalry Road EH11	031-337 3238	
Mill Warehouse (Murray Brothers)	14	F6
495 Lawnmarket EH1	031-225 9171	
Millshop	15	G5
53 George Street EH2	031-225 5464	
Millshop	14	F6
449 Lawnmarket EH1	031-220 1568	
Miss Selfridge	15	H5
13-21 Hanover Street EH2	031-220 1209	
Mondi	17	WU
U10 Upper Level, Waverley Shopping Centre EH1	031-556 3877	
Moss Bros	15	H5
43 George Street EH2	031-226 3016	
Mothercare	15	H6
84a Princes Street EH2	031-226 6503	
Next Directory	15	G6
74 Princes Street EH2	031-225 2756	
Next Originals	15	H6
14-16 Frederick Street EH2	031-225 4286	
Nickelby's	15	G6
94 Princes Street EH2	031-225 3140	
Number 2	16	F3
2 St Stephen Street EH3	031-225 2941	
Oasis	17	WL
L4 Lower Level,Waverley Shopping Centre EH1	031-556 4854	
Olympus Sport	15	H6
88 Princes Street EH2	031-225 3983	
Partners	13	H7
70-72 Grassmarket EH1	031-225 1885	

Thomas Pink	14	F5
32 Castle Street EH2	031-225 4264	
Principles	15	J5
16-17 Princes Street EH2	031-557 0120	
Private Lines	13	H7
86 Grassmarket EH1	031-226 7454	
Proudfoot	17	WU
U25 Upper Level, Waverley Shopping Centre EH1	031-556 0247	
Quick Stitch	14	G5
79 Rose Street EH2	031-225 5840	
Ragamuffin	44	L6
276 Canongate EH8	031-557 6007	
Razzle Dazzle	15	H6
63 Princes Street EH2	031-225 3264	
Richards	15	J5
46 Princes Street EH2	031-557 9499	
Rohan	14	G5
86 George Street EH2	031-225 4876	
Rosie's	42	J7
58 Candlemaker Row EH1	031-225 3055	
Russell & Bromley	42	G6
106 Princes Street EH2	031-225 7444	
School Exchange (above James Thin)	15	G5
57 George Street EH2	031-225 4495	
Sheepish Looks	13	H7
66 Grassmarket EH1	031-225 3249	
Simply Shetland	13	H8
9 West Port EH1	031-228 4578	
Skirt 'n' Slack Centre	14	F6
134 Princes Street EH2	031-225 5026	
Smith & Jones	17	WU
L3 Lower Level,Waverley Shopping Centre EH1	031-557 8834	
Sports Connection	14	F6
134A Princes Street EH2	031-225 3701	
Stewart, Christie & Co.	33	F5
63 Queen Street EH2	031-225 6639	
Swing	13	H7
60 Grassmarket EH1	031-226 7046	
Tee-Shirt Print	17	WL
L18 Lower Level,Waverley Shopping Centre EH1	031-557 2802	
Tenacious Hide	27	K3
71 Broughton Street EH1	031-557 8370	
Tie Rack	14	F6
134B Princes Street EH2	031-225 6955	
Tie Rack	17	WU
U20a Upper Level, Waverley Shopping Centre EH1	031-556 2622	
Tiso	14	G5
115-123 Rose Street EH2	031-225 9486	
Topsy Turvy	40	D7
18 William Street EH3	031-225 2643	
Traders for Men	13	H8
83 Grassmarket EH1	031-225 2476	
Vincent & Grant	14	F6
161a Rose Street EH2	031-220 3168	
Viyella	14	F6
128a Princes Street EH2	031-225 4652	
Wallis	14	F6
122 Princes Street EH2	031-225 3060	
Warehouse	17	WU
U9 Upper Level, Waverley Shopping Centre EH1	031-556 2770	
Who's Who	40	E6
23 Shandwick Place EH2	031-229 6998	
Wilkie's	40	E7
49-61 Shandwick Place EH2	031-229 5333	

CONSULATES

Australia	15	H5
80 Hanover Street EH2	031-226 6271	
Belgium	32	E5
13 Charlotte Square EH2	031-220 1490	
Denmark	36	M4
4 Royal Terrace EH7	031-556 4263	
Finland	14	G5
56 George Street EH2	031-225 1295	
France	32	D5
11 Randolph Crescent EH3	031-225 7954	
Germany	38	B7
16 Eglinton Crescent EH12	031-337 2323	
Greece	15	H5
2 Thistle Court, Thistle Street EH2	031-225 6744	
Italy	40	D6
32 Melville Crescent EH3	031-226 3631	
Netherlands	25	G2
113 Dundas Street EH3	031-225 8494	
Norway	14	G5
86 George Street EH2	031-226 5701	
Spain	14	F5
63 North Castle Street EH2	031-220 1843	
United States	36	M5
3 Regent Terrace EH7	031-556 8315	

SIGHTS Museums, monuments & notable buildings

Brass Rubbing Centre	43	K6
Chalmers Close, Trinity Apse EH1	031-556 4364	
Bute House	32	E5
6 Princes Street EH2	-	
Camera Obscura / Outlook Tower	42	H7
Castlehill EH1	031-226 3709	
Canongate Tolbooth	44	L6
163 Canongate EH8	031-225 2424	
Catherine Sinclair Monument	32	E5
St Colme Street EH2	-	
City Observatory	35	L4
Calton Hill EH1	-	
Commonwealth Institute	40	E7
8 Rutland Square EH1	031-229 6668	
Edinburgh Castle	42	G7
1 Castlehill EH1	031-225 9846	
Fettes College	22	A1
Carrington Road EH4	031-332 2281	
Georgian House	32	E5
7 Charlotte Square EH2	031-225 2160	
Gladstone's Land	9	J7
483 Lawnmarket EH1	031-226 5856	
Greyfriars Bobby	43	J8
Candlemaker Row EH1	-	
Greyfriars Kirk	42	J8
Greyfriars Place EH1	031-225 1900	
Huntly House Museum	44	M6
142 Canongate EH8	031-225 2424 (225 1131 on Saturdays)	
John Knox's House	43	L6
43-45 High Street EH1	031-556 9579	
Lady Stair's House	9	J7
Lady Stair's Close EH1	031-225 2424	
Lamb's House	55	P23
Water Street EH6	-	
Mercat Cross	9	J7
High Street EH1	-	
Museum of Childhood	43	L6
42 High Street EH1	031-225 2424	
National Library	42	J7
George IV Bridge EH1	031-226 4531	
National Library Map Room	56	M12
33 Salisbury Place EH9	031-667 7848	
National Monument	36	M5
Calton Hill EH1	-	
Nelson Monument	36	L5
Calton Hill EH1	-	
New Town Conservation Centre	33	G4
13a Dundas Street EH3	031-557 5222	
Old Calton Cemetery	35	K5
Waterloo Place EH1	-	
Old College	43	K8
South Bridge EH1	031-667 1011	
Palace of Holyroodhouse	37	P5
Abbey Strand EH8	031-556 1096	
Parliament House	43	K7
2 Crewe Toll EH5	031-225 2595	
People's Story	44	M6
163 Canongate EH8	031-225 2424 x6638	
Robert Burns Monument	36	M5
Regent Road EH7	-	
Robert Louis Stevenson's house	33	G4
17 Heriot Row EH3	-	
Royal College of Surgeons	43	L8
Surgeons' Hall, Nicolson Street EH8	031-556 6206	
Royal Museum of Scotland	43	K7
Chambers Street EH1	031-225 7534	
St Bernard's Well	32	E4
Near Mackenzie Place EH3	-	
St Giles Church	43	J7
High Street EH1	031-225 5147	
Scotch Whisky Heritage Centre	42	H7
Castlehill EH1	031-220 0441	
Scott Monument	34	J6
East Princes Street Gardens EH2	-	
Scottish-American War Memorial	42	G6
Princes Street EH2	-	
South Leith Parish Church	55	P24
Constitution Street EH6	031-554 2578(Hall)	
Trinity House	55	P24
Great Junction Street EH6	-	
Tron Kirk	43	K6
Hunter Square EH1	-	
West Register House	40	E6
Charlotte Square EH2	031-556 6585	

HOTELS

Adam	39	C
19 Lansdowne Crescent EH12	031-337 114	
Adria	36	M
11-12 Royal Terrace EH7	031-556 787	
Afton Award Pending	40	(
6 Grosvenor Crescent EH12	031-225 703	
Ailsa Craig	36	M
24 Royal Terrace EH7	031-556 102	
Albany	35	H
39 Albany Street EH1	031-556 039	
Allison ⚜ ⚜ Commended	56	N
17 Mayfield Gardens EH9	031-667 804	
Argus ⚜ ⚜ ⚜ Commended	46	E
14 Coates Gardens EH12	031-337 615	
Arkle	38	E
41 Coates Gardens EH12	031-337 116	
Arthur's View	56	N
10 Mayfield Gardens EH9	031-667 346	
Balmoral	35	H
Princes Street EH2	031-556 241	
Beresford	38	E
32 Coates Gardens EH12	031-337 085	
Boisdale ⚜ ⚜ ⚜ Commended	46	E
9 Coates Gardens EH12	031-337 113	
Brunswick ⚜ ⚜ Commended	28	M
13 Brunswick Street EH7	031-556 123	
Cairn ⚜ ⚜ ⚜ Approved	28	L
10-18 Windsor Street EH7	031-557 017	
Caledonian ⚜ ⚜ ⚜ ⚜ Highly Commended	40	H
Princes Street EH2	031-225 243	
Carlton Highland ⚜ ⚜ ⚜ ⚜ Highly Commended	43	H
North Bridge EH1	031-556 727	
Channings	31	C
12-16 South Learmonth Gardens EH4	031-315 222	
Christopher North House ⚜ ⚜ ⚜ Commended	32	F
6 Gloucester Place EH3	031-225 272	
Claremont	26	J
15 Claremont Crescent EH7	031-556 148	
Clarendon ⚜ ⚜ ⚜	39	C
22 Grosvenor Street EH12	031-337 703	
Claymore ⚜ ⚜ Approved	36	M
6 Royal Terrace EH7	031-556 269	
Clifton	39	C
1 Clifton Terrace EH12	031-337 100	
Cumberland ⚜ ⚜ Commended	46	A
1 West Coates EH12	031-337 119	
Dean	31	D
10 Clarendon Crescent EH4	031-332 030	
Donmaree	56	N
21 Mayfield Gardens EH9	031-667 364	
Drummond Hotel	26	J
34 Drummond Place EH3	031-556 305	
Dunstane House	46	A
4 West Coates EH12	031-337 532	
Eglinton	38	B
29 Eglinton Crescent EH12	031-337 264	
George Hotel ⚜ ⚜ ⚜ ⚜ ⚜ Commended	15	H
21 George Street EH2	031-225 125	
Georgian	24	F
5-4 Dean Terrace EH4	031-332 452	
Glencairn ⚜ ⚜ Approved	33	F
19-21 Royal Circus EH3	031-225 521	
Glenora ⚜ Commended	39	C
14 Rosebery Crescent EH12	031-337 118	
Gloucester	32	F
10 Gloucester Place EH3	031-225 237	
Greens	38	B
24 Eglinton Crescent EH12	031-337 156	
Greenside	36	M
9 Royal Terrace EH7	031-557 002	
Halcyon Award Pending	36	M
8 Royal Terrace EH7	031-556 103	
Herald House ⚜ ⚜ ⚜ Approved	48	D
70 Grove Street EH3	031-228 232	
High Street Youth Hostel	43	K
8 Blackfriars Street EH1	031-557 398	
Hilton National	38	B
69 Belford Road EH4	031-332 254	
Howard ⚜ ⚜ ⚜ ⚜ Highly Commended	26	H
32-36 Great King Street EH3	031-557 350	
King James Thistle ⚜ ⚜ ⚜ ⚜ ⚜ Highly Commended	35	K
107 Leith Street EH1	031-556 011	
Lairg Award Pending	46	B
11 Coates Gardens EH12	031-337 105	

The Scottish Tourist Board's gradings ⚜ ⚜ to ⚜ ⚜ ⚜ ⚜ ⚜ indicate the hotel's level of facilities. Where the hotel is 'Approved', 'Commended' or 'Highly Commended' the STB's inspectors have noted an above average quality of service and facilities.

ANTIQUES

Unicorn Antiques — 25 G3
65 Dundas Street EH3 — 031-556 7176
Upstairs, Downstairs — 56 M11
21a Causewayside EH9 — 031-668 4136
West Bow Antiques — 13 H7
102 West Bow EH1 — 031-226 2852
Whytock & Reid — 30 B5
Sunbury House, Belford Mews EH4 — 031-226 4911
Mr Wood's Fossils — 13 J7
5 Cowgatehead EH1 — 031-220 1344
Worthington — 56 M12
180 Causewayside EH9 — 031-663 8110

TRAVEL & TOURISM, TICKETS

AA — 40 D6
18-22 Melville Street EH3 — 031-225 8464
American Express — 14 F6
139 Princes Street EH2 — 031-225 7881
Festival Box Office — 42 J6
21 Market Street EH7 — 031-225 5756
Fringe Box Office — 43 K7
180 High Street EH1 — 031-226 5138
Jazz Festival Office — 44 M6
116 Canongate EH8 — 031-557 1642
Scottish Tourist Board — 15 J5
23 Ravelston Terrace EH4 — 031-332 2433
Tattoo Booking Office — 43 J6
22 Market Street EH7 — 031-225 1188

CHEMISTS, BODY CARE

Body Shop — 15 H6
96 Princes Street EH2 — 031-556 2641
Body Shop — 17 WU
U11 Upper Level, Waverley Shopping Centre EH1 — 031-556 2641
Boots — 14 G6
101-103 Princes Street EH2 — 031-225 6397
Boots (late opening / Sunday dispensary) — 40 E6
48 Shandwick Place EH2 — 031-225 6757
Crabtree & Evelyn — 15 H5
4 Hanover Street EH2 — 031-226 2478
Glovers Homeopathic Pharmacy — 40 D8
190 Morrison Street EH3 — 031-229 7664
Greenfields — 24 E3
22 Raeburn Place EH4 — 031-332 7878
Health Call Medical Centre — 39 D6
11 Drumsheugh Gardens EH3 — 031-225 1341
Napier's — 43 J8
18 Bristo Place EH1 — 031-220 3981
Nectar Beauty — 17 WL
L1a Lower Level, Waverley Shopping Centre EH1 — 031-556 1321
Waverley Pharmacy — 17 WU
U2 Upper Level, Waverley Shopping Centre EH1 — 031-556 5023
Yves Rocher — 17 WU
U26 Upper Level, Waverley Shopping Centre EH1 — 031-557 5000

OUTDOORS, SPORTS, CYCLING

Jocky Allan — 55 P26
115 Leith Walk EH6 — 031-554 6698
Blues — 14 F5
1 Wemyss Place EH3 — 031-225 8369
Central Cycle Hire — 49 F10
13 Lochrin Place EH3 — 031-228 6333
City Cycles — 26 H1
30 Rodney Street EH7 — 031-557 2801
Cycles — 56 M11
12 West Preston Street EH8 — 031-667 8473
John Dickson — 15 G5
21 Frederick Street EH2 — 031-225 4218
Edinburgh Golf Centre — 47 C8
58 Dalry Road EH11 — 031-337 5888
Elliott Sports — 56 M11
57-9 South Clerk Street EH8 — 031-668 1098
Lothian Ski Services — 26 H1
50 Rodney Street EH7 — 031-557 9072
MacDonald, W.R. — 40 F8
26 Morrison Street EH3 — 031-229 8473
New Bikes — 49 F9
14 Lochrin Place EH3 — 031-228 6363
Outdoors — 47 C8
28 Dalry Road EH11 — 031-337 6360
Quarterback — 49 G9
2 Brougham Place EH3 — 031-229 2736
Royal Commonwealth Pool — 56 N11
21 Dalkeith Road EH16 — 031-667 7211
Secondhand Bike Shop — 29 N1
29 Iona Street EH6 — 031-553 1130
Shooting Lines — 52 M10
18 Hope Park Terrace EH9 — 031-668 3746
Sportswide — 52 L9
80 Nicolson Street EH8 — 031-668 1564

Stirlingshire Saddlery — 39
230-232 Morrison Street EH3 — 031-229 8[
Wind Things — 13
11 Cowgatehead EH1 — 031-220 6[

FOOD and DRINK

Baxters — 14
122-124 Rose Street EH2 — 031-226 2[
Better Beverage Co. — 39
43 William Street EH3 — 031-226 6[
Chocolats et Lollipops — 24
45 Raeburn Place EH4 — 031-315 2[
Di Placido — 24
4 St Mary's Street EH1 — 031-557 4[
Edinburgh Organic Shop — 49
132 Lauriston Place EH3 — 031-228 34
Justerini & Brooks — 15
39 George Street EH2 — 031-226 4[
Maxwell & Kennedy — 15
95 Princes Street EH2 — 031-220 04
Maxwell & Kennedy — 17
L16 Lower Level, Waverley Shopping Centre EH1 — 031-558 1[
Natures Gate — 52
83 Clerk Street EH8 — 031-668 2[
Real Foods — 49
8 Brougham Street EH3 — 031-228 1[
Stuarts Sweets — 43
5 Cockburn Street EH1 — 031-220 3[
Thorntons — 14
116 Princes Street EH2 — 031-225 1[
Whisky Shop — 17
L2b Lower Level, Waverley Shopping Centre EH1 — 031-558 1[
T.G. Willis & Co Ltd — 14
135 George Street EH2 — 031-225 2[

INTERIOR DESIGN, FURNISHINGS, HOUSEHOL[

Athena — 17
U30 Upper Level, Waverley Shopping Centre EH1 — 031-556 24
Azteca — 13
16 Victoria Street EH1 — 031-226 66
Burning Question — 33
19B Howe Street EH3 — 031-55742[
Copperknob — 15
3 Frederick Street EH2 — 031-220 67
Robert Cresser — 13
40 Victoria Street EH1 — 031-225 2[
A.F.Drysdale — 16
35 & 20 North West Circus Place EH3 — 031-225 46
Dunedin Interiors — 16
4 North West Circus Place EH3 — 031-220 10
Ettrick Forrest Design — 44
254 Canongate EH8 — 031-556 22
Fast Feathers — 49
14 Leven Street EH3 — 031-228 12
Flowers by Maxwell — 14
32B Castle Street EH2 — 031-226 28
Habitat — 40
32 Shandwick Place EH2 — 031-220 9[
Harriet's House — 16
74 St Stephen Street EH3 — 031-220 62
Inhouse — 33
28 Howe Street EH3 — 031-225 28
Inscape — 34
26 Dublin Street EH3 — 031-557 55
Liberty — 15
47 George Street EH2 — 031-226 54
Lonsdale & Dutch — 33
23B Howe Street EH3 — 031-556 32
Iain Mackie — 24
71 Raeburn Place EH4 — 031-332 40
Marks & Spencer (household) — 14
53 Princes Street EH2 — 031-225 23
Material World — 33
4 Howe Street EH3 — 031-220 48
Mary Maxwell — 26
31A Dublin Street EH3 — 031-557 21
Sarah Menzies — 56
166-88 Causewayside EH9 — 031-668 22
Pavilion — 33
6A Howe Street EH3 — 031-225 35
Quadrant — 16
5 North West Circus Place EH3 — 031-226 72
Ross Cookshop — 17
L7 Lower Level, Waverley Shopping Centre EH1 — 031-557 40

CRAFTS and GIFTS

Adam Pottery — 25
76 Henderson Row EH3 — 031-557 39
Bear's Den — 42
51 George IV Bridge EH1 — 031-220 12

Casa Fina	**15**	**H4**
107 Hanover Street EH2	031-225 2022	
Coleridge	**15**	**G5**
47B George Street EH2	031-220 1305	
Craft Centre	**17**	**WL**
L9 Lower Level,Waverley Shopping Centre EH1	031-556 9370	
Different Things	**17**	**WU**
U18 Upper Level, Waverley Shopping Centre EH1	031-556 9199	
Digger	**51**	**K8**
38 West Nicolson Street EH8	031-668 1802	
Embroidery Shop	**39**	**D7**
51 William Street EH3	031-225 8642	
Finishing Touch	**52**	**L9**
134 Nicolson Street EH8	031-667 0914	
Frasers & Son	**17**	**WL**
L2a Lower Level,Waverley Shopping Centre EH1	031-557 3875	
Gallery Dolls & Dolls' Hospital	**34**	**H3**
35a Dundas Street EH3	031-556 4295	
Glassmarket	**43**	**L6**
25 Jeffrey Street EH1	031-557 3517	
Great Northern Wood	**17**	**WL**
L5b Lower Level,Waverley Shopping Centre EH1	031-557 8098	
Henderson Artshop	**24**	**E2**
28A Raeburn Place EH4	031-332 7800	
Images of Nepal	**13**	**H7**
10 Grassmarket EH1	031-220 4208	
Indo-Thai	**51**	**K9**
47 West Nicolson Street EH8	031-667 8200	
Joe Cool	**14**	**G6**
16 Rose Street EH2	031-556 7153	
Loco	**13**	**H7**
98 West Bow EH1	031-226 7460	
Macdonald Nelson Trading Co.	**13**	**H7**
34 Victoria Street EH1	031-225 2672	
Nostalgia Shop	**43**	**J8**
13 Forrest Road EH1	031-226 4353	
The Owl & the Pussycat	**17**	**WL**
L1b Lower Level,Waverley Shopping Centre EH1	031-557 4420	
Paper Tiger	**41**	**F7**
53 Lothian Road EH1	031-228 2790	
Paper Tiger	**40**	**E6**
10-16 Stafford Street EH3	031-226 5812	
Papertree	**14**	**G5**
93 Rose Street EH2	031-220 3734	
Partytime	**24**	**D3**
63 Raeburn Place EH4	031-332 2261	
Poppy's Gifts	**14**	**F6**
133 Rose Street EH2	031-220 1281	
Presence	**17**	**WL**
L8 Lower Level,Waverley Shopping Centre EH1	031-556 3818	
Quercus	**33**	**F4**
16 Howe Street EH3	031-220 0147	
Round the World	**13**	**J7**
82 West Bow EH1	031-225 7086	
Route Sixty Six	**14**	**G5**
107-109 Rose Street EH2	031-225 5962	
Score Commotions	**13**	**H7**
99 West Bow EH1	031-225 2034	
Scotrocks	**13**	**H7**
10 Grassmarket EH1	031-226 6383	
Something Else	**40**	**E6**
4 Drumsheugh Place EH3	031-220 1013	
Stockwell China Bazaar	**17**	**WU**
U15 Upper Level, Waverley Shopping Centre EH1	031-556 1181	
Studio One	**40**	**D7**
10-14 Stafford Street EH3	031-226 5812	
Walrus & Carpenter	**39**	**D7**
34 William Street EH3	031-226 3934	
Ware on Earth	**33**	**G4**
15 Howe Street EH3	031-558 1276	
West Bow Needle Art	**13**	**H7**
93 West Bow EH1	031-220 0373	
Ye Old Curiosity Shoppe	**13**	**H7**
25 West Bow EH1	031-225 3902	
Ye Olde Christmas Shoppe	**36**	**M6**
145 Canongate EH8	031-557 9220	

DEPARTMENT STORES and AUCTION ROOMS

BHS	**15**	**H6**
64 Princes Street EH2	031-226 2621	
Debenhams	**14**	**G6**
109-112 Princes Street EH2	031-225 1320	
Frasers	**40**	**E6**
145 Princes Street EH2	031-225 2472	
Jenners	**15**	**J5**
48 Princes Street EH2	031-225 2442	
John Lewis	**35**	**K4**
69 St James Centre EH1	031-556 9121	
Junior Jenners	**15**	**H5**
21 Rose Street EH2	031-225 2442	

Littlewoods	**15**	**H6**
91 Princes Street EH2	031-225 1683	
Lyon & Turnbull	**15**	**G5**
51 George Street EH2	031-225 4627	
Marks & Spencer	**15**	**H5**
53 Princes Street EH2	031-225 2301	
Newkirkgate Shopping Centre	**55**	**P24**
Great Junction Street EH6	-	
Phillips	**15**	**G5**
65 George Street EH2	031-225 2266	
Sotheby's	**14**	**F6**
112 George Street EH2	031-226 7201	
Waverley Shopping Centre	**15**	**J5**
Waverley Market EH1	-	

MEDIA, INSTITUTIONS

BBC	**34**	**H4**
5 Queen Street EH2	031-225 3131	
General Register for Births, Deaths & Marriages	**15**	**J5**
New Register House, West Register Street EH2	031-334 0380	
Grampian TV	**39**	**D7**
6 Manor Place EH3	031-226 3926	
Radio Forth	**35**	**K3**
13-17 Forth Street EH1	031-556 9255	
Scottish Record Office	**15**	**J5**
2 Princes Street EH2	031-556 6585	
Scottish TV, Gateway Studio	**28**	**M2**
42 Elm Row EH7	031-557 4554	
Student Advice Place	**51**	**K8**
16 Potterrow EH8	031-668 2834	

MUSIC, ELECTRICAL and PHOTOGRAPHIC

Coda Music	**17**	**WU**
U14 Upper Level, Waverley Shopping Centre EH1	031-557 4694	
Carl Dyson	**17**	**WU**
U29 Upper Level, Waverley Shopping Centre EH1	031-557 2917	
Dixons	**14**	**F6**
130 Princes Street EH2	031-226 3711	
Focal Point	**17**	**WL**
L5a Lower Level,Waverley Shopping Centre EH1	031-556 3907	
Gordon Simpson	**40**	**E7**
6a Stafford Street EH3	031-225 6305	
HMV	**14**	**F6**
129 Princes Street EH2	031-226 3466	
Virgin Megastore	**14**	**F6**
131 Princes Street EH2	031-225 4583	
GD Young Cameras	**39**	**D8**
250 Morrison Street EH3	031-229 6601	

JEWELLERY and ACCESSORIES

Clarksons	**13**	**H7**
87 West Bow EH1	031-225 8141	
Gullivers	**17**	**WU**
U3 Upper Level, Waverley Shopping Centre EH1	031-556 3659	
Hamilton & Inches	**14**	**G5**
87 George Street EH2	031-225 4898	
Harlequin Jewellers	**17**	**WL**
L17 Lower Level,Waverley Shopping Centre EH1	031-557 1319	
Mappin & Webb	**14**	**G5**
88 George Street EH2	031-225 5502	
Ringmaker	**17**	**WU**
U19 Upper Level, Waverley Shopping Centre EH1	031-557 6711	
Torq	**15**	**H5**
80a Princes Street EH2	031-220 6976	

HOBBIES and MODELS

Harburn Hobbies	**28**	**M2**
67 Elm Row EH7	031-556 3233	
Mac's Models	**44**	**M6**
133-5 Canongate EH8	031-557 5551	
Royal Mile Miniatures	**44**	**M6**
154 Canongate EH8	031-557 2293	

MISCELLANEOUS

Astrology Centre	**16**	**F3**
60 St Stephen Street EH3	031-225 2779	
Byzantium (Diverse covered market)	**13**	**J7**
9a Victoria Street EH1	031-225 1768	
California Tan	**16**	**F3**
66 St Stephen Street EH3	031-220 2045	
Edinburgh Shaver Centre	**33**	**G5**
39 Queen Street EH2	031-220 1594	
Kinnaird (Cooperage)	**40**	**E6**
2 Victoria Dock (near The Shore)	031-553 7624	
Herbert Love (Tobacco)	**40**	**E6**
31 Queensferry Street EH2	031-225 8082	
Marco's and Little Marco's (Health Club)	**48**	**E9**
51-95 Grove Street EH3	031-228 2141	
Steiner Hairdressing	**17**	**WU**
U17 Upper Level, Waverley Shopping Centre EH1	031-556 7788	

STREET INDEX

The figures and letters after a street name indicate the page number (**in bold**) and map square where the name will be found.
The figures and letters directly following a street name indicate the postal district of the entry.

Abbreviations:
RBG – Royal Botanic Gardens
WU - Waverley Shopping Centre Upper Floor
WL - Waverley Shopping Centre Lower Floor